PHILOSOPHERS

First published in 1993 by
Cornerhouse Publications
70 Oxford Street
Manchester M1 5NH  England
061 228 7621



ISBN 0 948797 76 2

Prints: Steve Pyke, Vince Goodsell & Gordon MacDonald
Design and Artwork Production: Cornerhouse
Reprographics: Leeds Photo Litho
Print: Jackson Wilson

Printed on Sky Special Matt 150 gsm & 300 gsm

The staff at Cornerhouse for Philosophers are:
Dewi Lewis, Director
Niall Allsop, Design & Producton
Stephanie Laidler & Angela Bradley, Production Assistants
Alison Buchan & Katherine Pearce, Sales & Distribution

A complete catalogue of Cornerhouse Publications
is available on request

"The critical attitude may be described as the conscious attempt to make our theories, our conjectures, suffer in our stead in the struggle for the survival of the fittest. It gives us a chance to survive the elimination of an inadequate hypothesis, when a more dogmatic attitude would eliminate it by eliminating us."

Sir Karl Popper

# PHILOSOPHERS

## STEVE PYKE

Dear Sam,
All the best to you and Mitzi in the years ahead.
Yours ever,
Mark Sheridan

C

For Nichola

When Steve Pyke asked me to write an introduction to his book of photographs of philosophers, I was at once flattered and slightly dismayed to be associated with what, by any reckoning, must rank as one of the major achievements in the field of portraiture in recent years. But what could I write about portraits so direct and so pure, and about eighty philosophers of whom I knew next to nothing?

When Pyke then followed up his request with several pages of notes, it was clear that his own words had an authenticity and immediacy with which I could not hope to compete. We therefore decided to sit down together and from this came the short interview which follows.

Portrait photographers have long seemed to me a foolhardy breed, hoping to capture not just the appearance but the spirit of their subject in a fraction of a second on an extremely small and flat surface. The photographs in this book prove that this is not only possible but that the results can be both profound and moving.

Pyke whose education has been in the school of life rather than in the university has tackled here a potentially awesome subject instinctively and with great commitment. Arguments about whether photography is or is not an 'art' so obviously fall apart when confronted with this kind of energy and vision. These photographs provide the most vivid introduction possible to some of the greatest minds of our age.

Robin Gibson
National Portrait Gallery

Steve Pyke interviewed by Robin Gibson, 1 September 1993

**Robin Gibson**  What gave you the idea of doing a series of portraits of philosophers?

**Steve Pyke**  The Philosophers began as a result of a commission to photograph Sir A J Ayer for a magazine in October 1988. The fifteen minutes I had been told I could expect with him turned into three fascinating hours. He talked about all sorts of things, including philosophy. Some time later when I looked back on this meeting, I realised how influential it had been in setting this body of work in motion. It seemed a natural path to take with my photography.

**RG**  Had you done a project like this before? Were you looking for a project at the time?

**SP**  At this point I was particularly interested in working on an extended body of work. The previous two years has been spent working fairly intensively for magazines; turnaround and deadline times are very short. Although I had always set aside time for my own work, I wanted to work on something more involving.

**RG**  How did you go about finding out which philosophers you should photograph?

**SP**  Not being a philosopher or an academic meant that I could not choose my sitters. I asked each philosopher I photographed to choose ten living formative influences. The first three philosophers I went to see I asked for their choice of ten and I was given twenty three names. At first, very, very few names came up twice. It was at that point that I realised this was going to become a long term project. I had no idea what the philosophers would look like before I met them. These people are not known for their faces but for their ideas. It's a collection of people brought together by their individual ways of perceiving the world.

**RG**  Did the project gather momentum as you went along or was there a point at which you might have abandoned it?

**SP**  The collection happened almost without me realising it. At the beginning I imagined I would end up with maybe ten photographs; but within the first month I'd photographed around thirty different philosophers. I would say that I act intuitively. I rarely dissect or take apart my reasons for doing something – it's difficult for me to say why. Things happen in a certain way at a certain time and in a way it became compulsive. Given a different set of events I would have become inspired to photograph more of the *Homeless* series. It was a period of exploration.

**RG**  Most of the portraits are taken in your full-frame close-up format. When did you first start using this format? How are the photographs taken?

**SP**  The first close-up I shot was Sam Fuller, the film director in 1983. I use a Rolleiflex 2.8f camera with Rolleinor close-up attachments. Basically what I thought was interesting was that these allow me to photograph within two feet of the subject. I'm close enough to touch the sitter within what's usually considered their own personal space. It's a space that people only share with the people they feel close to. I photograph against a black or white background: it's like a large five foot square pillowcase I got my grandmother to make. With the exception of one frame (Tzvetan Todorov) all the photographs are shot in natural light. I find it more sensitive.

**RG**  What effect do you think this has on the portraits?

**SP**  I've always felt it's quite an honest way of photographing people. People become very concentrated and very aware, sometimes uneasy at what I'm doing. For me the result is much more 'focussed'.

**RG**  Does the book include all the philosophers you have photographed? Is the project complete?

**SP**  There are philosophers who chose not to be photographed and the book contains no Eastern philosopher. Some I have not had the chance to meet yet, but it is a body of work I intend to continue. This book is a document of people – philosophers who are regarded by their peers as the foremost thinkers of our age.

**RG**  What did you hope to achieve by asking each philosopher to write a short piece to accompany the photograph?

**SP**  By asking philosophers to write a hundred words to describe their 'philosophy' I hoped to give an insight into the thoughts which they have devoted their lives to. In some ways I feel this demystifies philosophy. Before I started this project philosophy was to me like magic, a world accessible only to a few.

**RG**  Do you think there are features in these photographs which indicate what all the subjects have in common – I mean that they are all philosophers?

**SP**  I have no influence over how people choose to interpret my photographs. I only know that because these are pictures of people who have concentrated on their thoughts as a way of life, it in turn raises many interesting questions about ways of seeing. If my way of seeing makes you think about such things then this can only be towards better understanding in general. Photography and philosophy are different ways of perceiving the world.

**RG**  I found when I was looking through the portraits that I was starting to distinguish between the sitters who (I thought) had reacted to you as a person or perhaps to what you were saying or doing at the time (the one of Phillipa Foot is particularly memorable from this point of view), and those where the sitters are perhaps reacting in a conventional way to having their photograph taken, plus a few who might actually have been slightly hostile. Are you aware of this when you're going through the contacts?

**SP**  What you carry away from a portrait session is the memory of the person. What happens when you go through the contacts is that this memory affects your edit. The time I spent with Phillipa Foot, I remember that of the sixty minutes we spent in conversation, I was only photographing her for perhaps ten. It's the sixty minutes that have an effect on my final image – either in the way she responds to camera or in the way she responds to me. I expect every sitter to react differently to my photographs. How they react and what they reveal is what I find so stimulating. I see my life's work as photographing the human face and don't believe I will ever tire of it.

**Professor Elizabeth Anscombe**

*Cambridge, 15 May 1990*

"Much of my work has been concerned with intention. Like any object an action has many descriptions true of it; under some it is intentional. But not all the intentions which an agent thinks an action of his falls under are in fact true of it. For example we all mean to do well for ourselves but that doesn't mean we do."

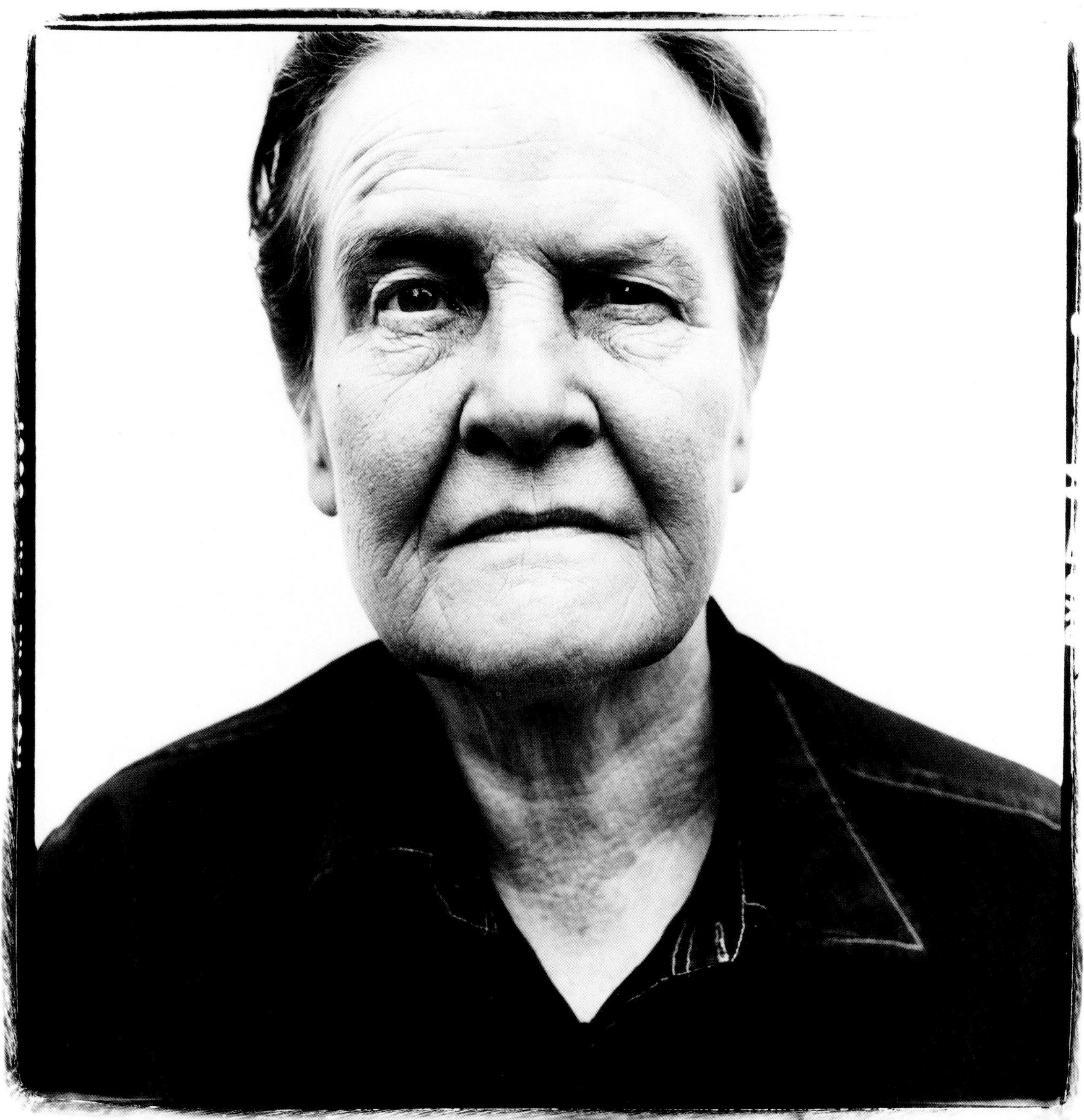

**Professor David Armstrong**

*London, 15 June 1990*

D M Armstrong has worked on perception, on the mind-body problem, on the theory of knowledge and, latterly, on fundamental problems about the general nature of what is. He sees man as an evolved creature and the world as a spacetime manifold governed by the laws of physics. His political and social instincts lead him to seek a compromise between liberalism and conservatism.

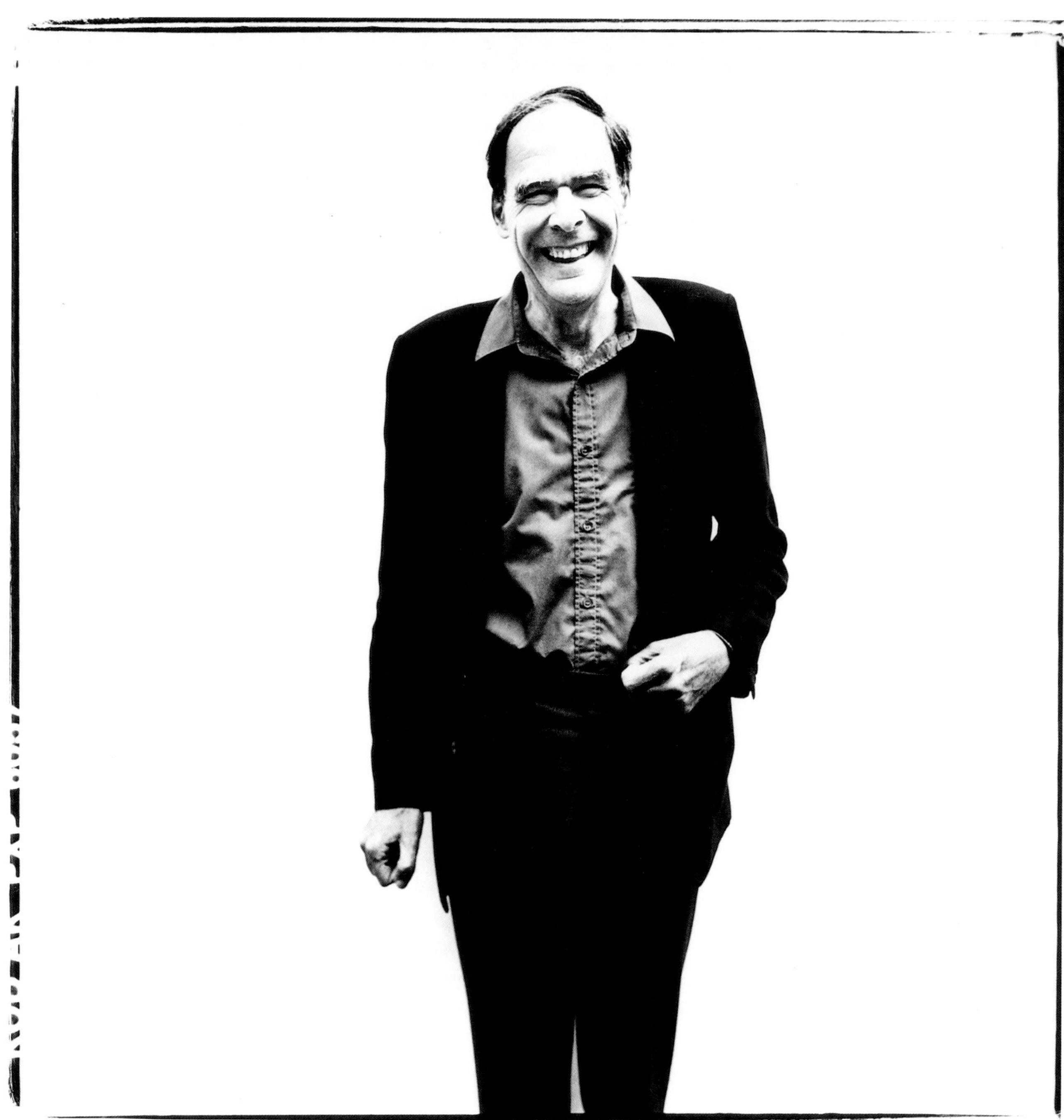

**Professor Sir Alfred Ayer**

*London, 5 October 1988*

Professor Sir Alfred Ayer – Freddie to all who knew him, and to many who didn't – was born in 1910 and became the very best known and among the few most distinguished of British philosophers. His first book, Language, Truth and Logic, was published in 1936, and became the bible of Logical Positivism in the English Language. It contributed greatly to the character and temper of the best philosophy of ensuing decades. He subsequently wrote The Problems of Knowledge, which he sometimes took to be his best book, and many other philosophical works. He was Grote Professor of the Philosophy of Mind and Logic at University College London and Wykeham Professor of Logic at Oxford. He died on 27 June 1989. *Ted Honderich*

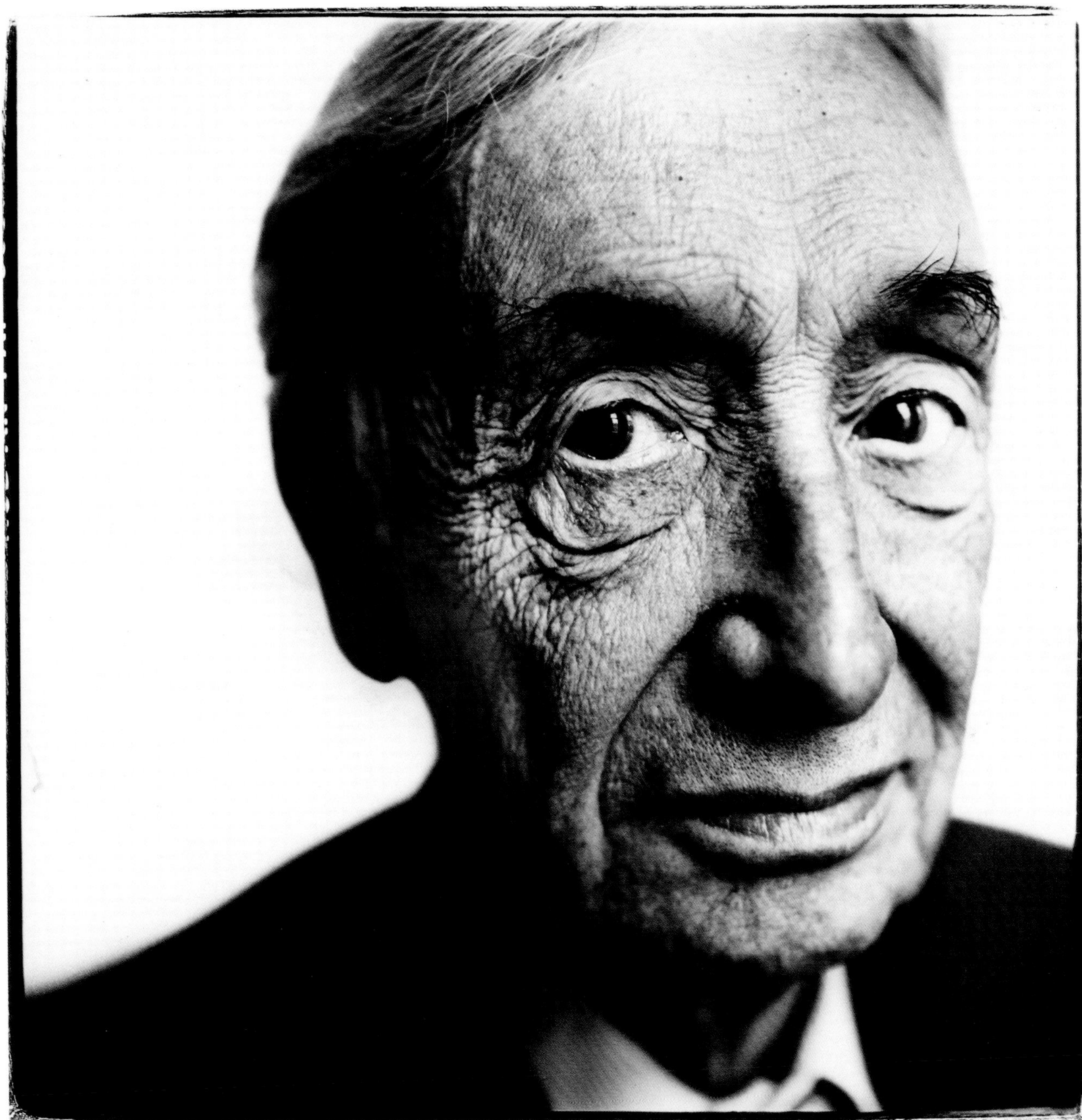

**Professor Jonathan Barnes**

*Oxford, 7 June 1990*

"In ethics, a sceptical hedonism.

In politics, a conservative anarchism.

In metaphysics, all for Aristotle and common sense.

In epistemology, unreconstructed empiricism.

In logic-logic.

Most of the half-truths of philosophy were half-known to the Greeks. The chief task of modern philosophy is – or should be – to protect these truths against the ever-flowing tide of folly and superstition and cant."

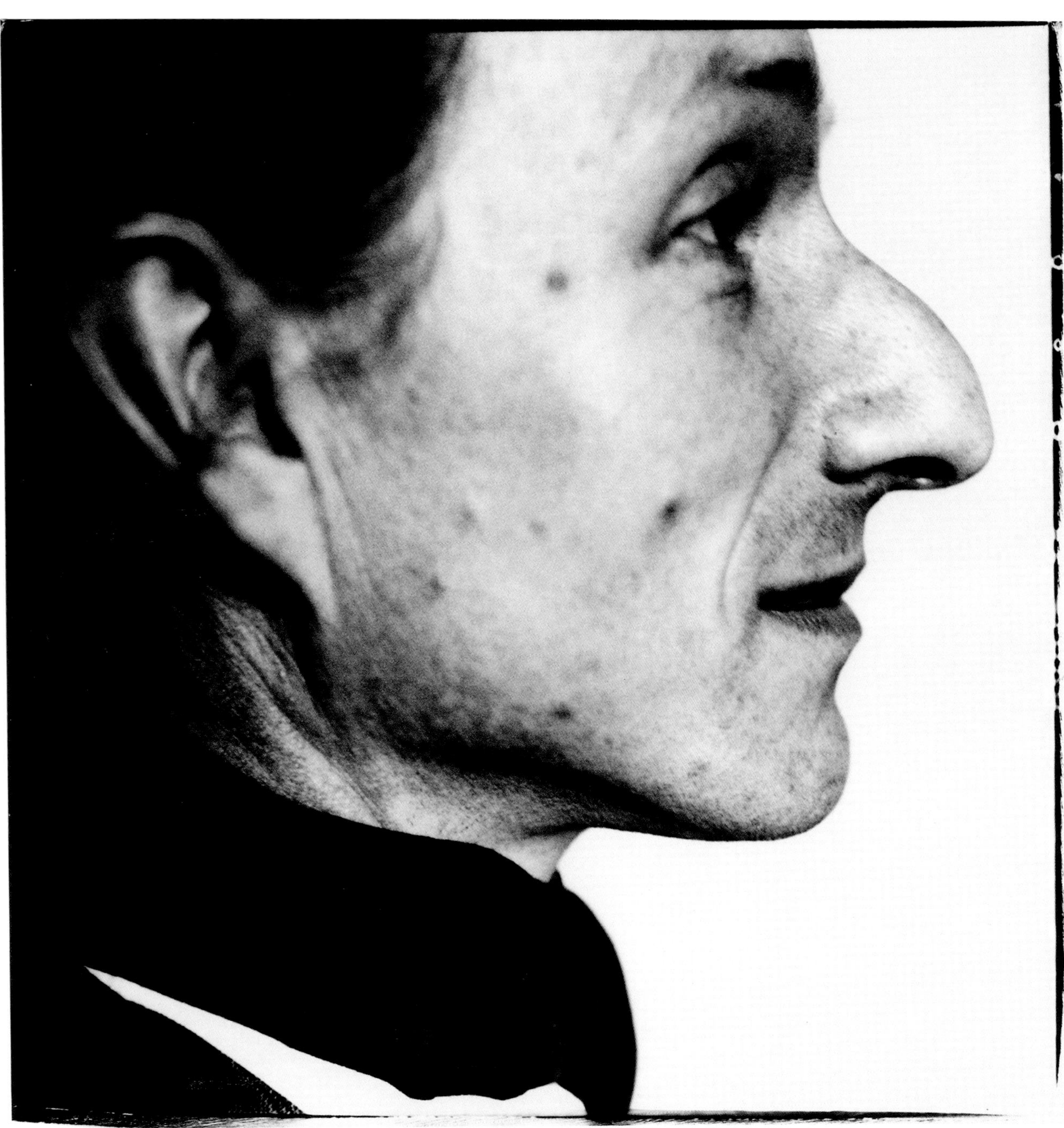

**Professeur Jean Baudrillard**

*Paris, 6 December 1991*

"The form of my language is almost more important than what I have to say within it.
Language has to be synchronous with the fragmentary nature of reality. With its viral, fractal
quality, that's the essence of the thing! It's not a question of ideas – there are already too
many ideas!"

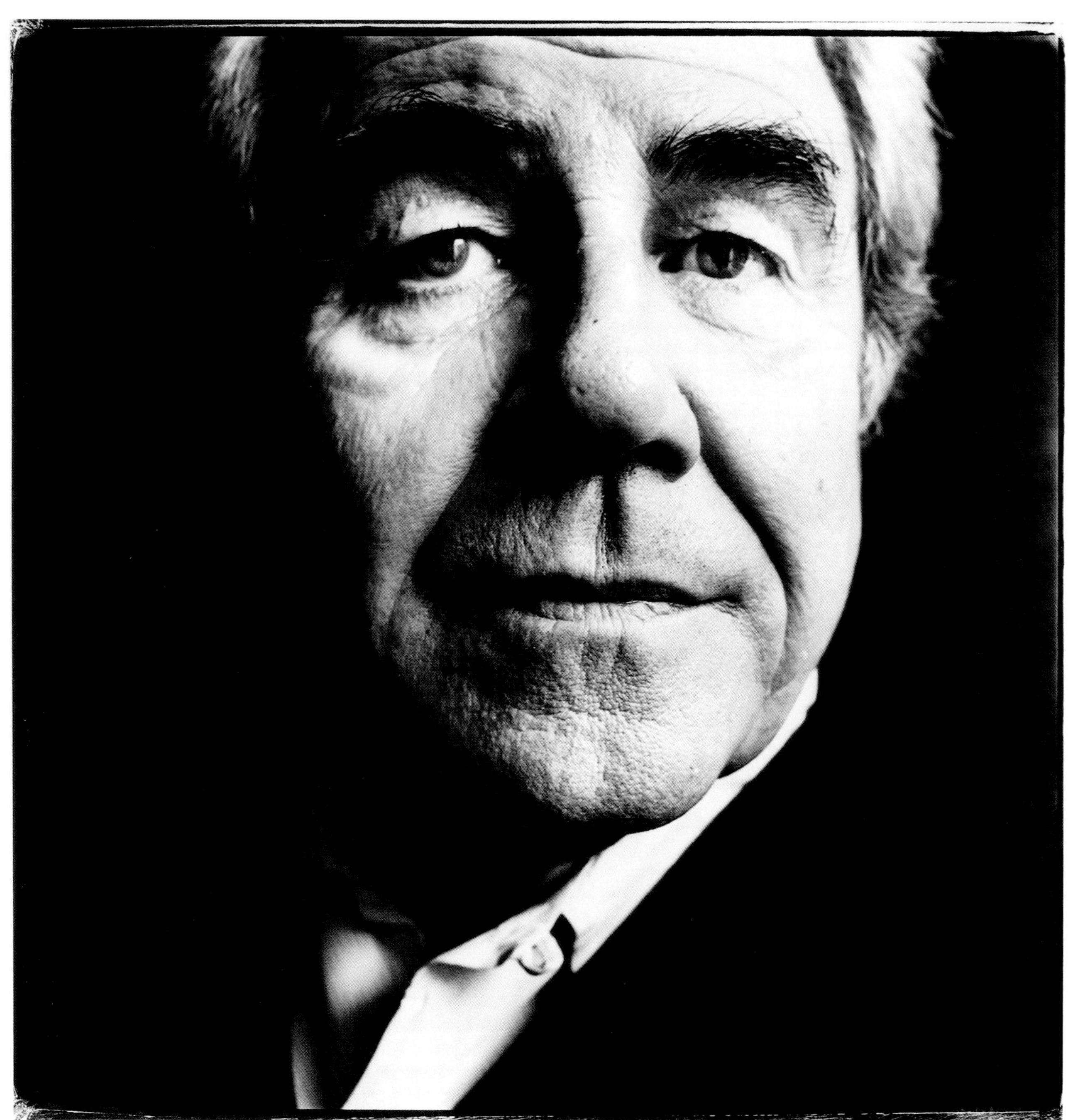

**Sir Isaiah Berlin**

*London, 14 June 1990*

"Men cannot live without seeking to describe and explain the universe to themselves. The models they use in doing this must deeply affect their lives, not least when they are unconscious; much of the misery and frustration of men is due to the mechanical and unconscious, as well as deliberate, application of models where they do not work... The goal of philosophy is always the same, to assist men to understand themselves and thus operate in the open and not wildly, in the dark."

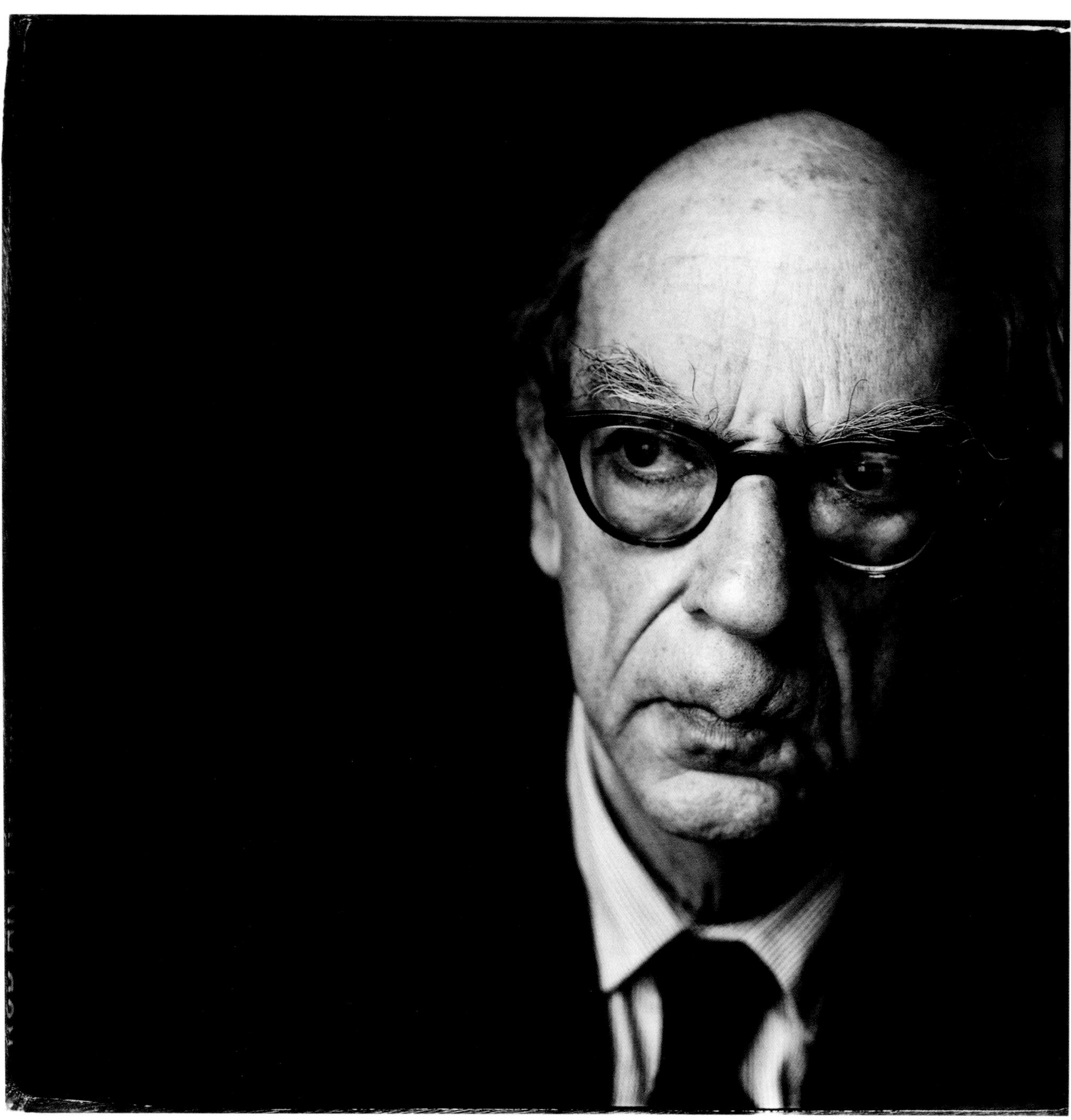

**Dr Simon Blackburn**

*Oxford, 7 June 1990*

"Philosophy is the disciplined study of the major categories of thought: truth, proof, experience, knowledge, mind and matter. In it the general concepts making the framework in which we think of things are themselves made into the objects of study. It has no boundaries, so that a philosopher might as easily find himself engaging with the arguments of Plato or Hume as with those of contemporary writers; it has no set menu of techniques, so that one common topic of philosophical debate is that of the best way to pursue such studies. Some schools have found the key to lie in language, others in the philosophy of mind, others in trying to benefit from the advances of empirical science."

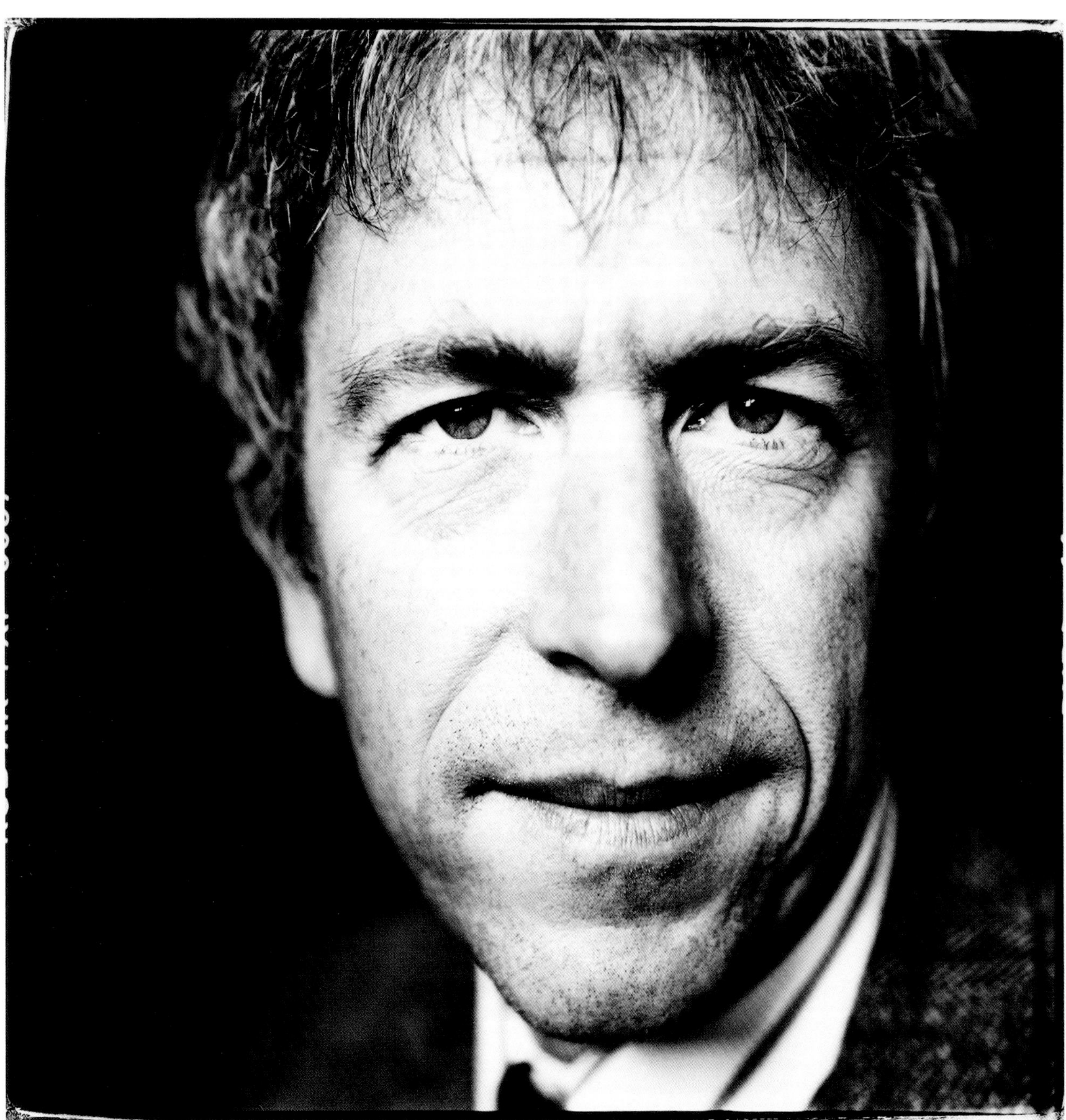

**Professeur Jacques Bouveresse**

*Paris, 12 September 1990*

False philosophers: they are the ones created by the teaching of philosophy, the programs.
They learn the problems that they would not have discovered by themselves and that they
don't feel. They learn all of them [the problems].
The very true problems of the true philosophers are those that harass and embarrass life —
which does not mean that they are absurd. But at least they are alive and are true as
sensations. *Paul Valéry from 'Mauvaises pensées et autres' … Bad thoughts and others*

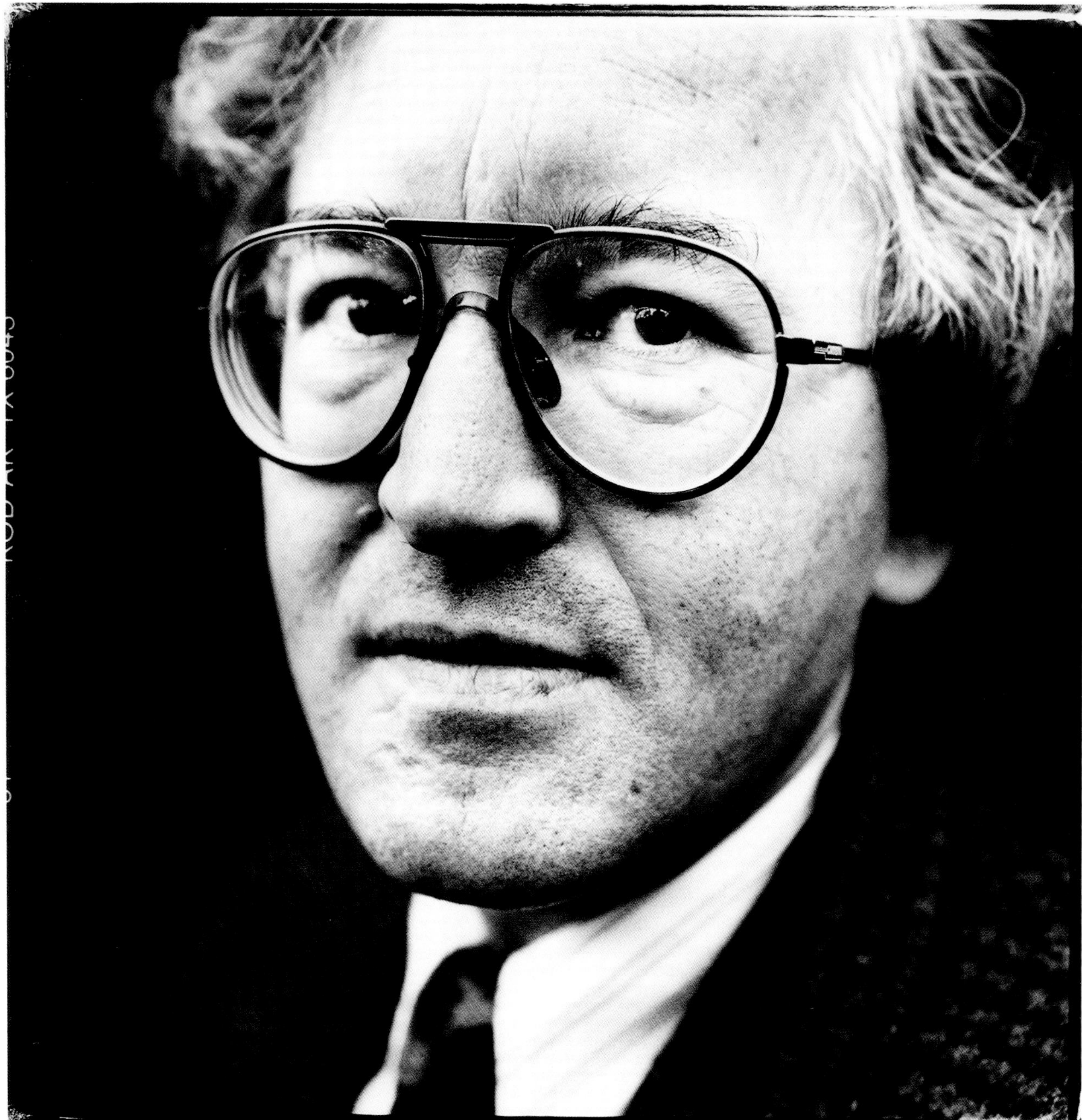

**Professor Miles Burnyeat**

*Cambridge, 22 June 1992*

Miles Burnyeat was studying Greek and Latin at school when, at the age of 16, he was bowled over by A J Ayer's *Language, Truth and Logic*. The school banned the book because it said that religious statements are cognitively meaningless; he stayed torn between Classics and Philosophy. Then came National Service in the Royal Navy, delightfully spent learning to be a Russian Interpreter, after which he went to Cambridge and discovered that much of the best philosophy is written in Greek and Latin. All it needs is interpretation, in a style that is sensitive both to its original cultural context and to the concerns of modern philosophy. So he has spent his life interpreting ancient philosophy to modern audiences. In 1984 he became Laurence Professor of Ancient Philosophy at Cambridge University. His book *The Theaetetus of Plato* was published in 1990.

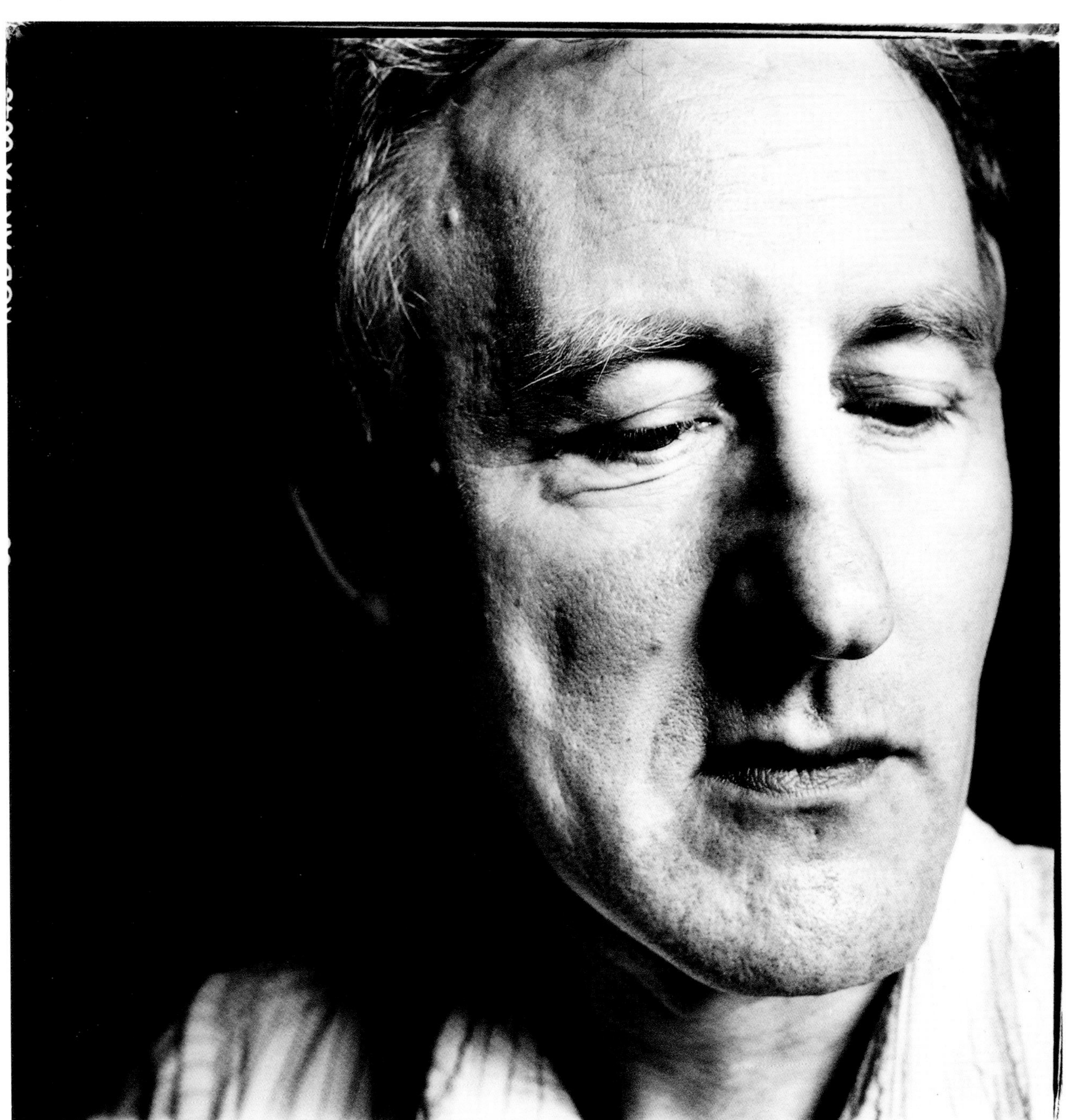

**Professor John Campbell**

*Cambridge, 15 May 1990*

"Philosophy is thinking in slow motion. It breaks down, describes and assesses moves we ordinarily make at great speed – to do with our natural motivations and beliefs. It then becomes evident that alternatives are possible."

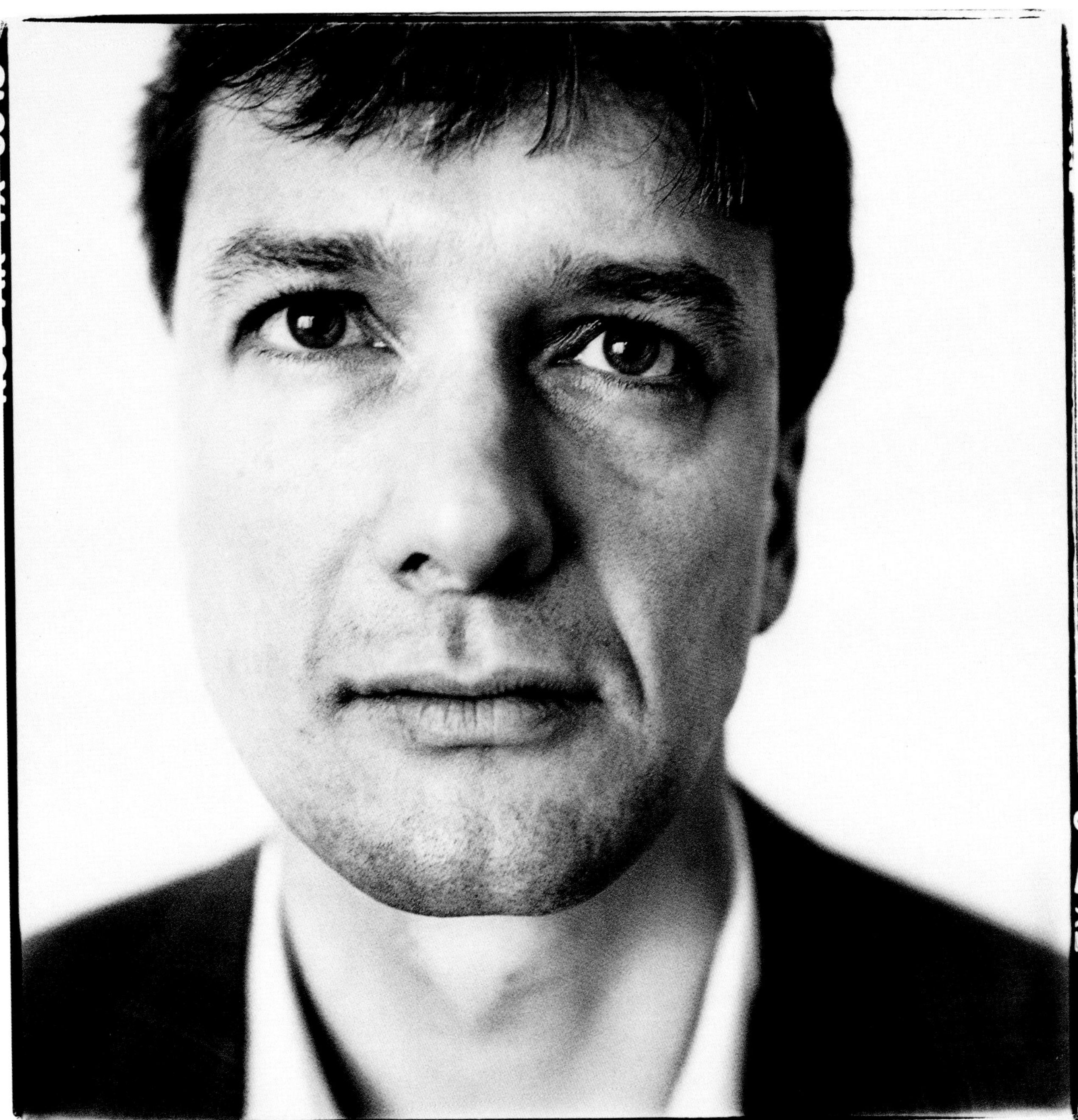

**Professor Nancy Cartwright**

*Oxford, 5 July 1990*

"Philosophy should be founded on detailed, positive knowledge of actual processes in the world
and not on abstract assessments of human capacities."

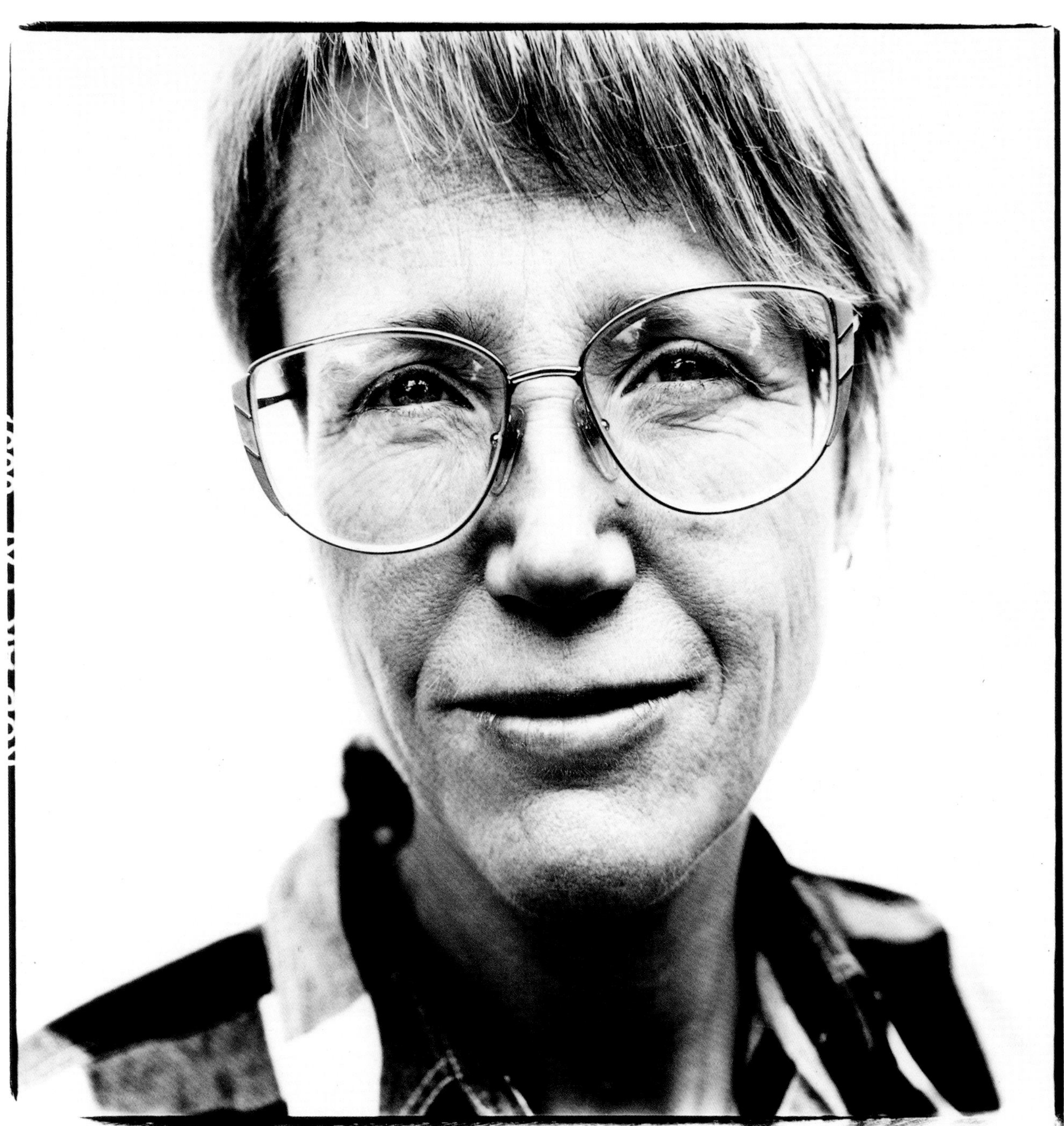

**Nirad Chaudhuri**

*Oxford, 9 May 1990*

"I was never a Professor or a professional philosopher. My 'philosophy' is for my personal use, and it has, so far served me well."

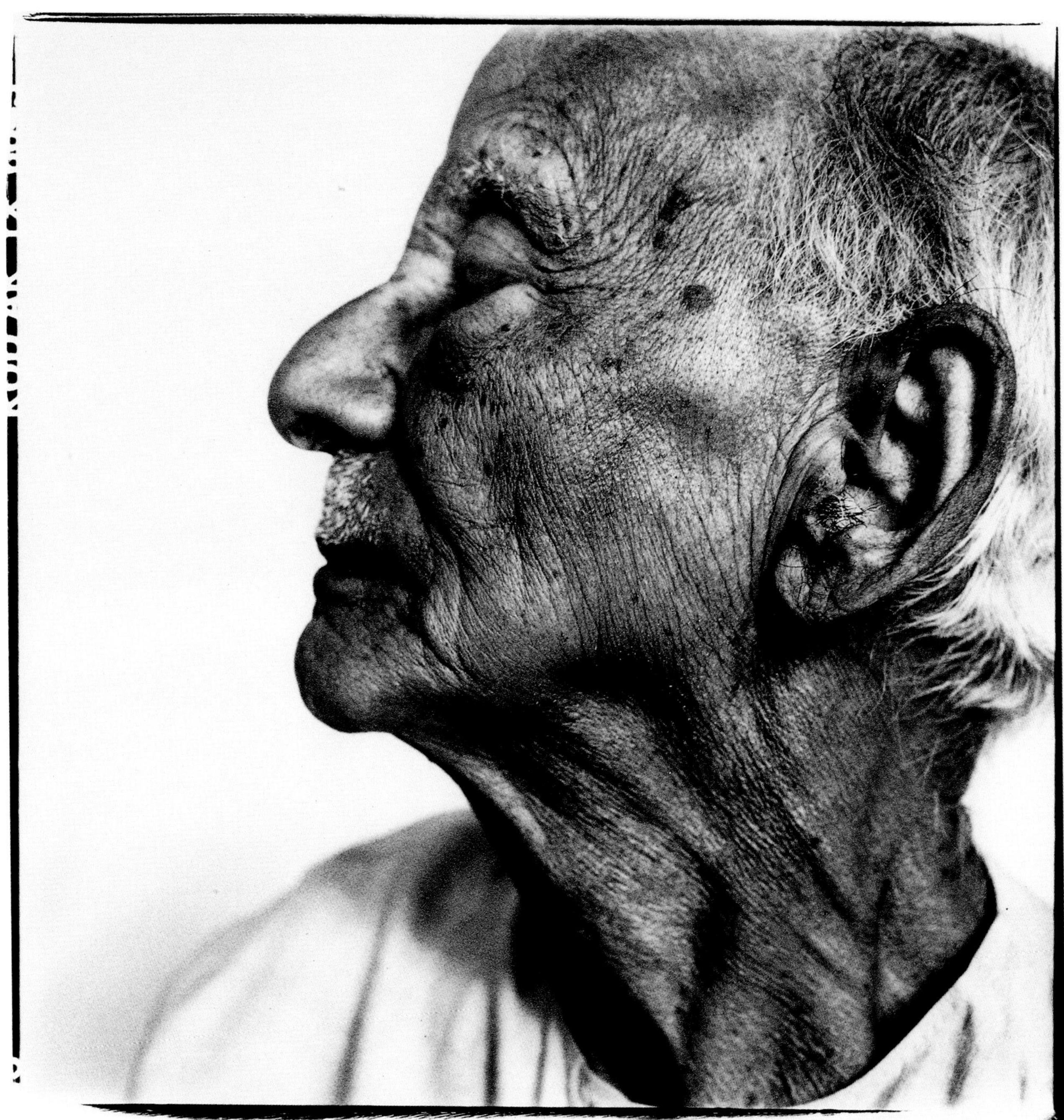

**Professor Noam Chomsky**

*Boston, 29 May 1990*

"A number of the leading questions in philosophy can, I think, be profitably formulated and addressed from a naturalistic perspective that derives in thrust, if not in content, from the early modern period. That has been my primary interest, particularly as regards topics concerning language and mind, the biological roots of human understanding and language as a modality for expression of thought."

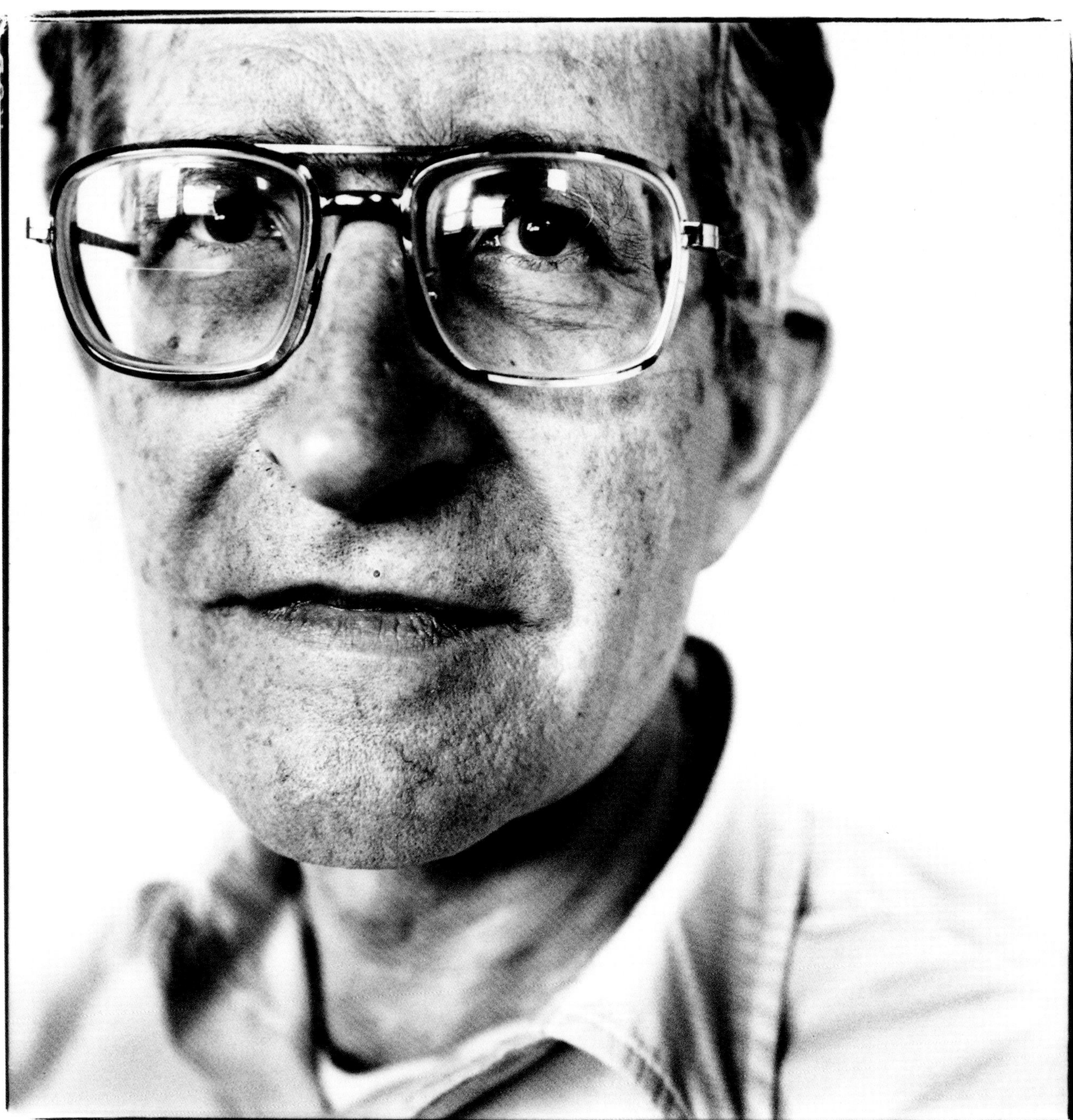

**Professor Gerry Cohen**

*London, 8 June 1990*

"I devoted many years to thinking about the materialist conception of history, and I published the results of that reflection in Karl Marx's *Theory of History: A Defence* (Oxford, 1978). The book was part of what came to be known as Analytical Marxism, a school of thought in which rigorous methods are applied in the pursuit of Marxist themes.

More recently, I have been studying the concepts of freedom and justice as they bear on the great political choice of our epoch: between capitalist and socialist forms of society. I am on the socialist side of the divide, and I seek to address the intellectual and historical challenges that socialism currently faces."

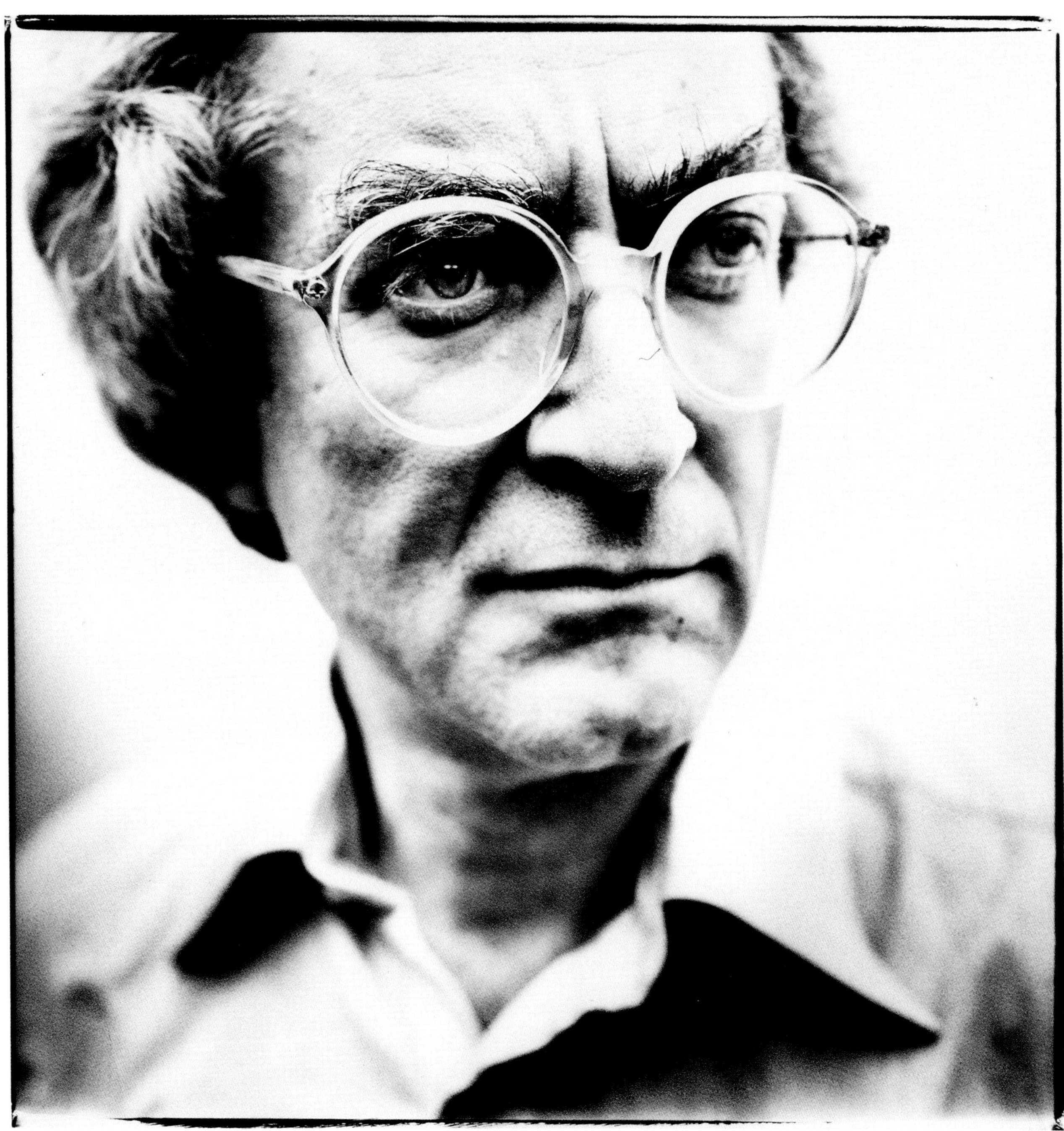

**Professor Donald Davidson**

*Santa Cruz, 24 July 1990*

"Gertrude Stein said of someone, 'He is a village explainer. This is fine if you are a village; if not, not.' I have always wanted to be a village explainer, but for the most part I do not think I have succeeded: my writing has been found dense and difficult. It is a troubling sign that people cannot decide where to file me. I have been called a realist and an anti-realist, an internalist and an externalist, a subjectivist and an objectivist, a materialist, a monist and an epiphenomenalist. My theory of action has been tagged a causal theory, and I have been accused of making the mental causally impotent. I confess I am responsible for wrongly labelling my view of truth both a correspondence theory and a coherence theory (it is neither), and Richard Roty says I am pragmatist. But I am not completely discouraged: if you are a village, I will keep on trying to explain myself."

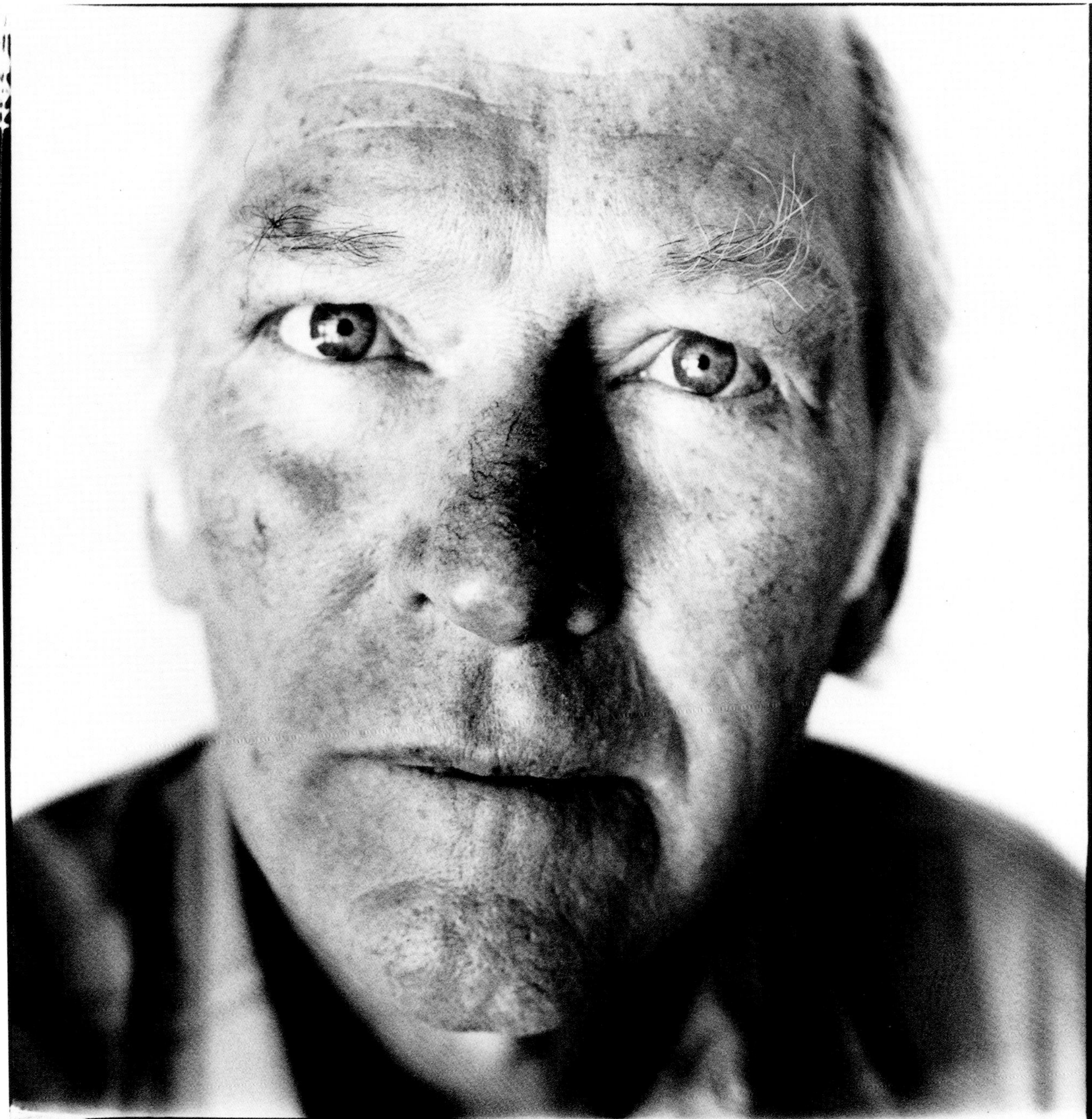

**Professor Daniel C Dennett**

*London, 9 March 1992*

"What you can imagine depends on what you know. Philosophers who know only philosophy consign themselves to a janitorial role in the great enterprises of exploration that are illuminating the mysteries of our lives."

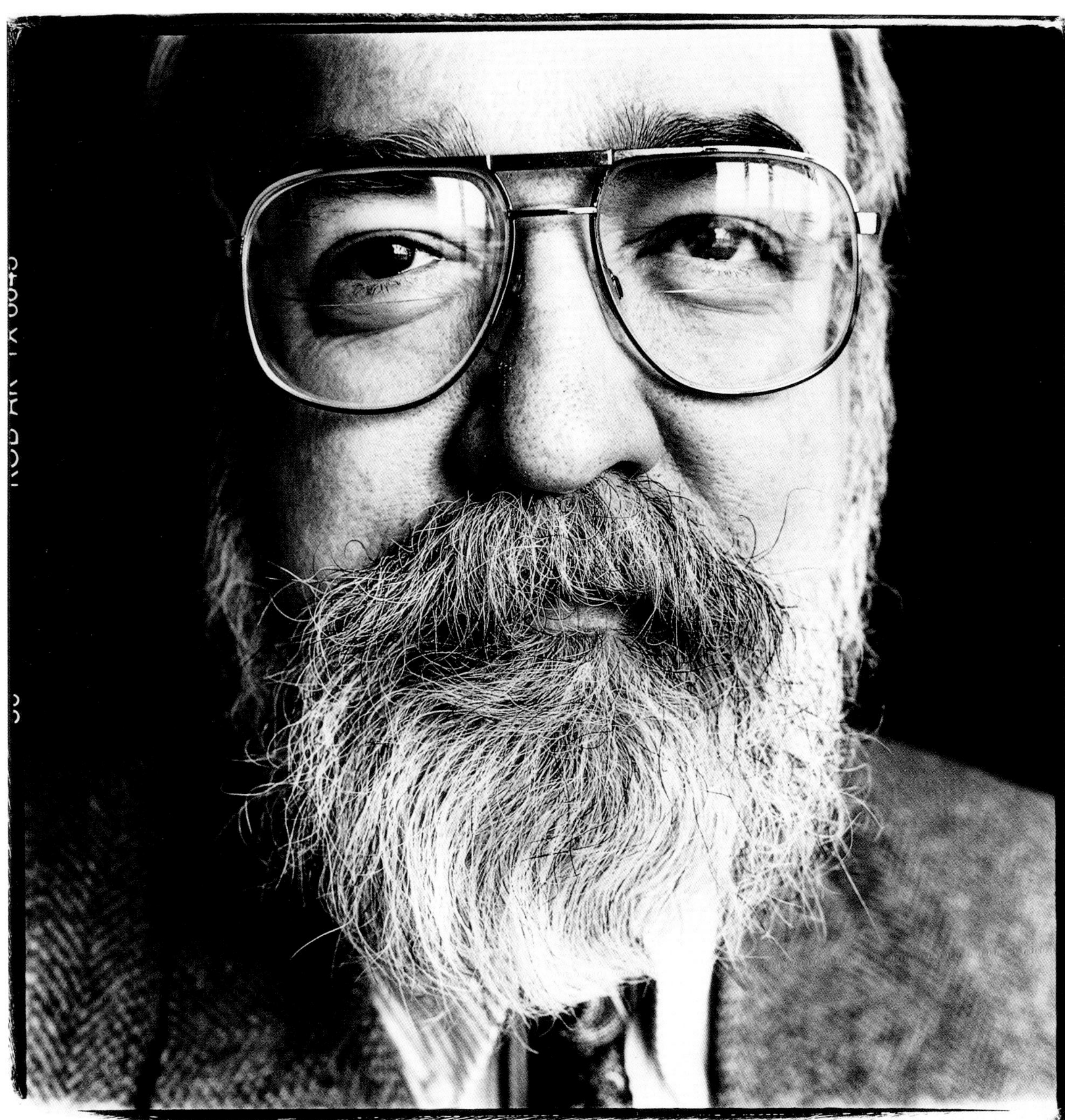

**Professeur Jacques Derrida**

*Paris, 12 September 1990*

"The philosopher should start by meditating on photography, that is to say the writing of light
before setting out towards a reflection on an impossible self-portrait."

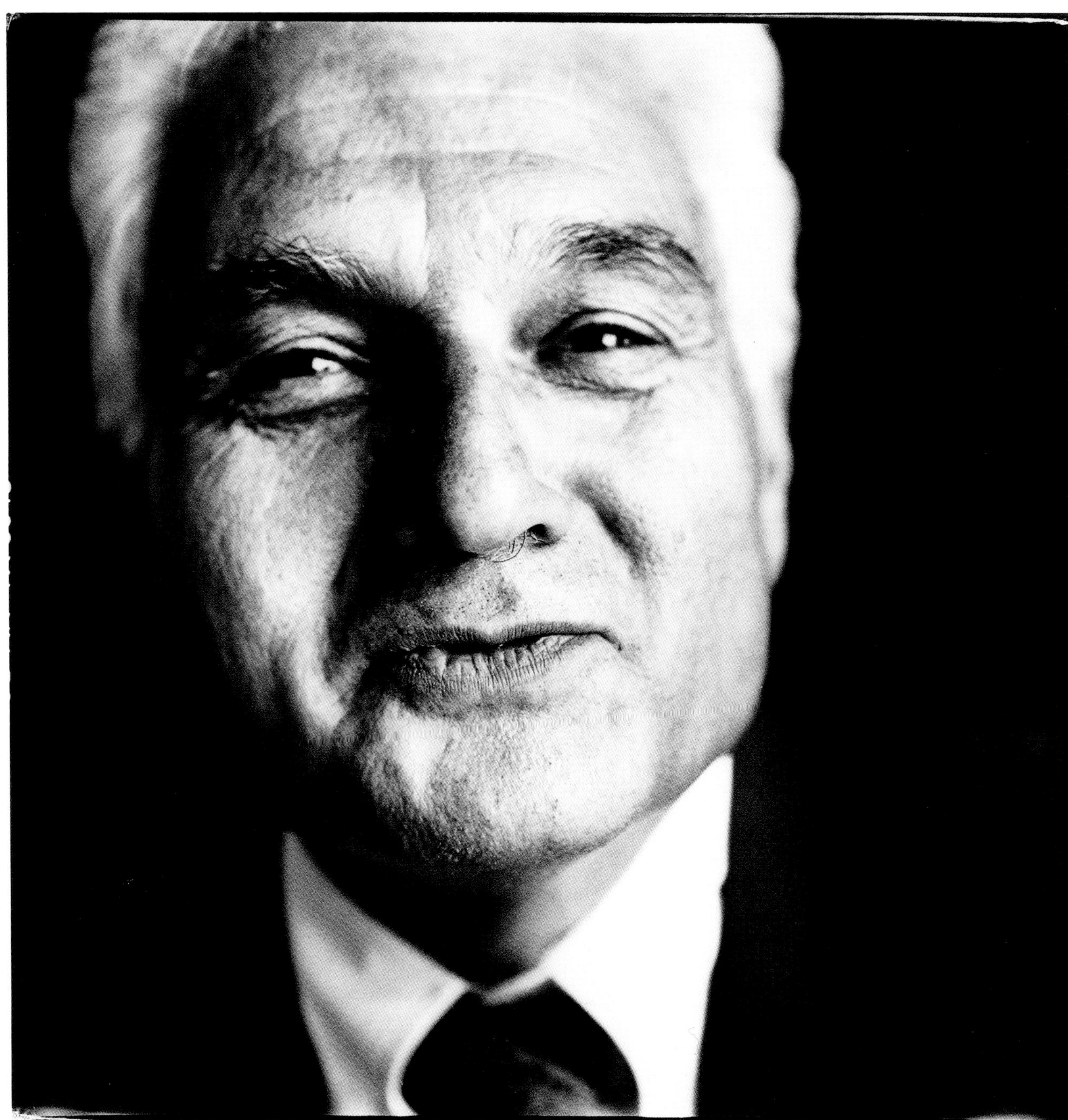

**Professor Michael Dummett**

*Oxford, 21 May 1990*

"Philosophy attempts, not to discover new truths about the world, but to gain a clear view of
what we already know and believe about it. That depends upon attaining a more explicit grasp
of the structure of our thoughts; and that in turn on discovering how to give a systematic
account of the working of language, the medium in which we express our thoughts."

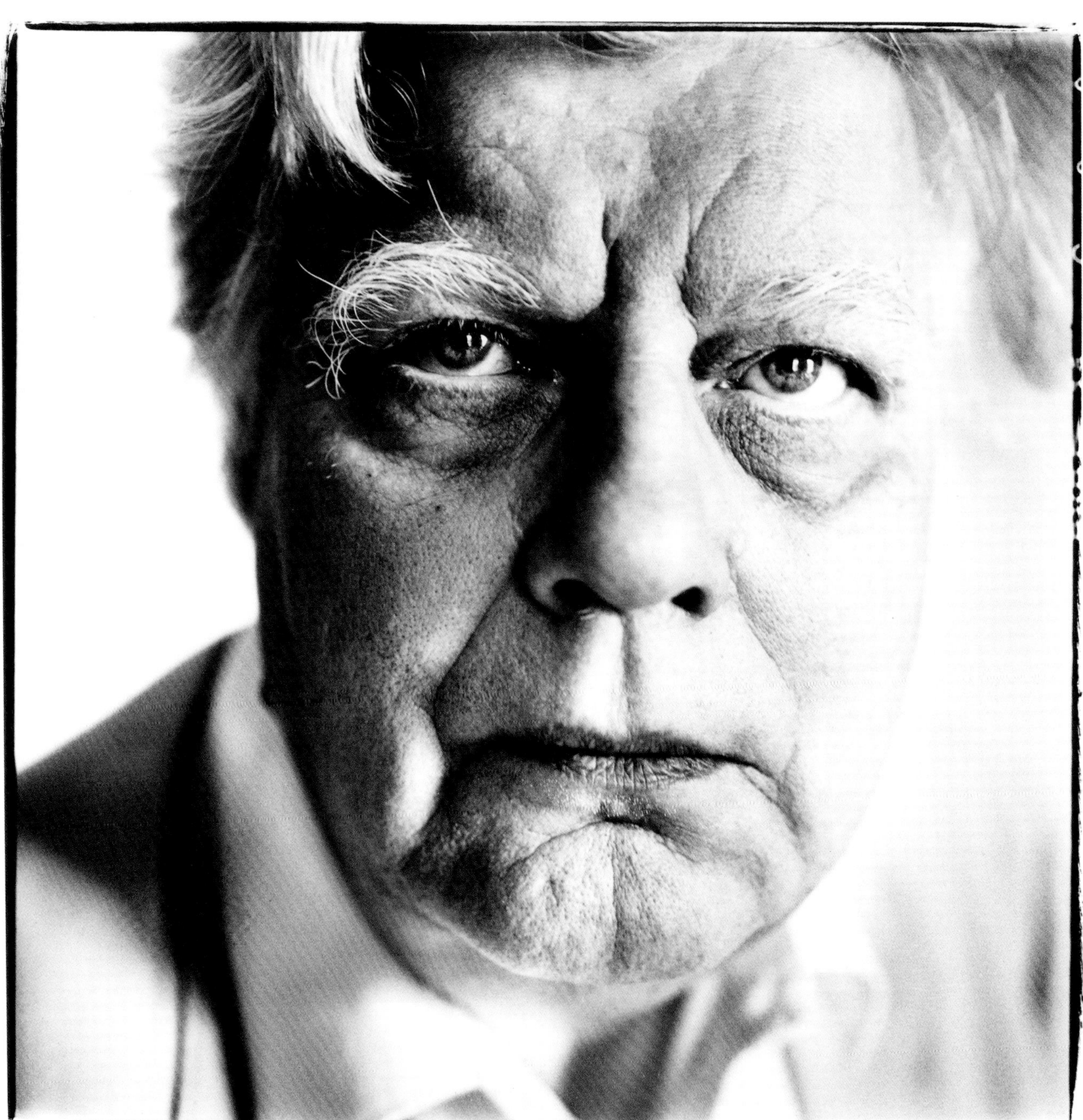

**Professor Ronald Dworkin**

*London, 1 May 1992*

"There is no canonical philosophical method any more than there is a canonical photographic style, in both cases method is part of what is created. But my own preference is for philosophy from the inside out – beginning in very concrete moral or political or legal controversies or puzzles and confronting only the general theoretical issues we see we need to confront to think sensibly about those concrete controversies. I prefer that to philosophy from the outside in, which begins in general theory, and seeks practical application later. In both cases philosophical issues of great abstraction, depth and difficulty must eventually be reached, either at the beginning or at the end. The difference is rather in how the abstract issues are chosen, combined and formulated. When we reason from the outside in, practical issues must shop from among ready-made philosophical theories waiting on the racks to see which asks and tries to answer questions that best fit its own dimensions. When we reason from the inside out, those theories are bespoke, made for the occasion, Saville Row, not Seventh Avenue."

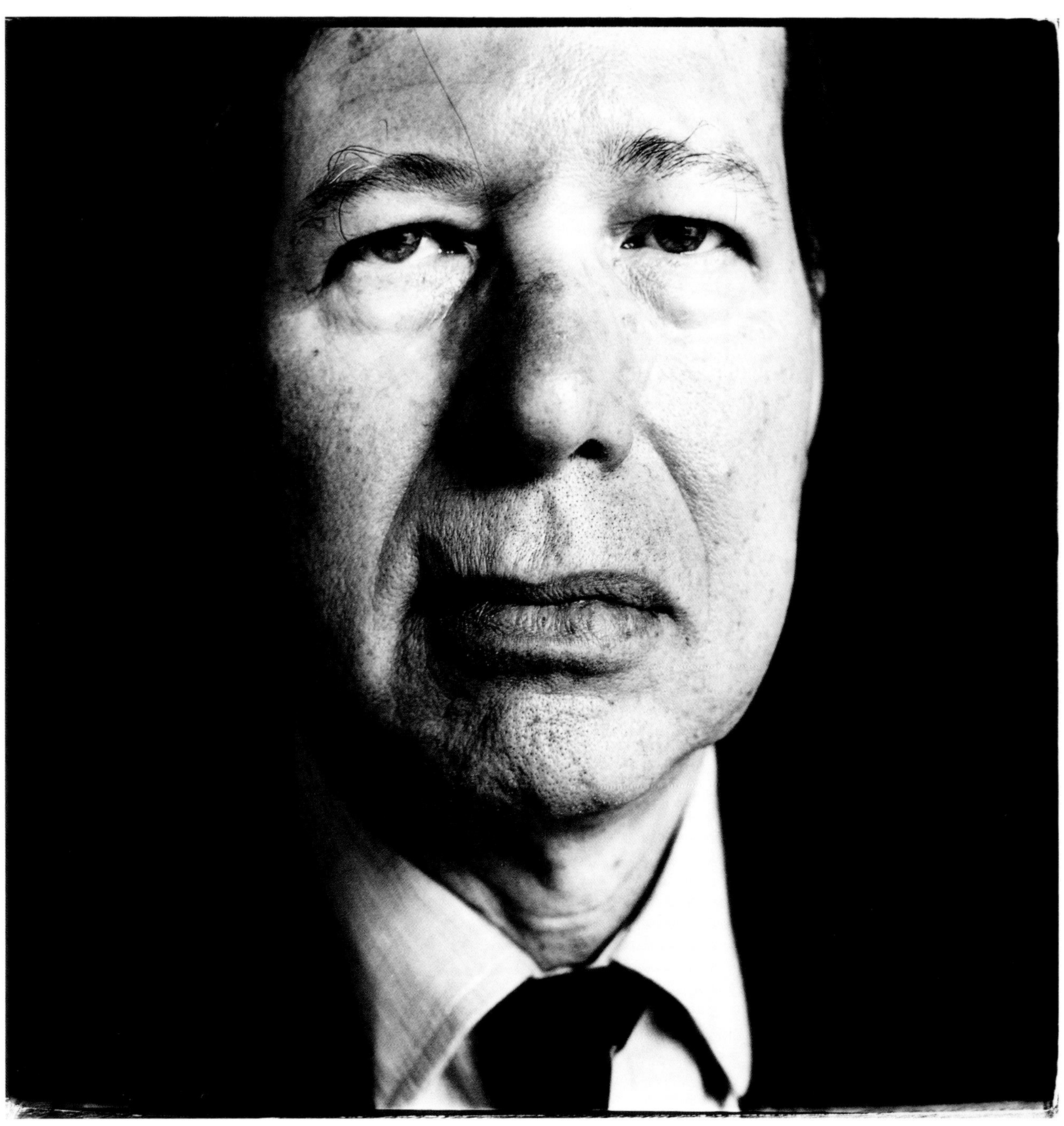

**Professor Dorothy Emmet**

*Cambridge, 22 June 1992*

"I am interested in religion, morals, politics, and broadly what the world is like, and want to be clearer about what to think. I can't say as much as I thought I could but what I can means more. I enjoy other philosophers whether or not we agree."

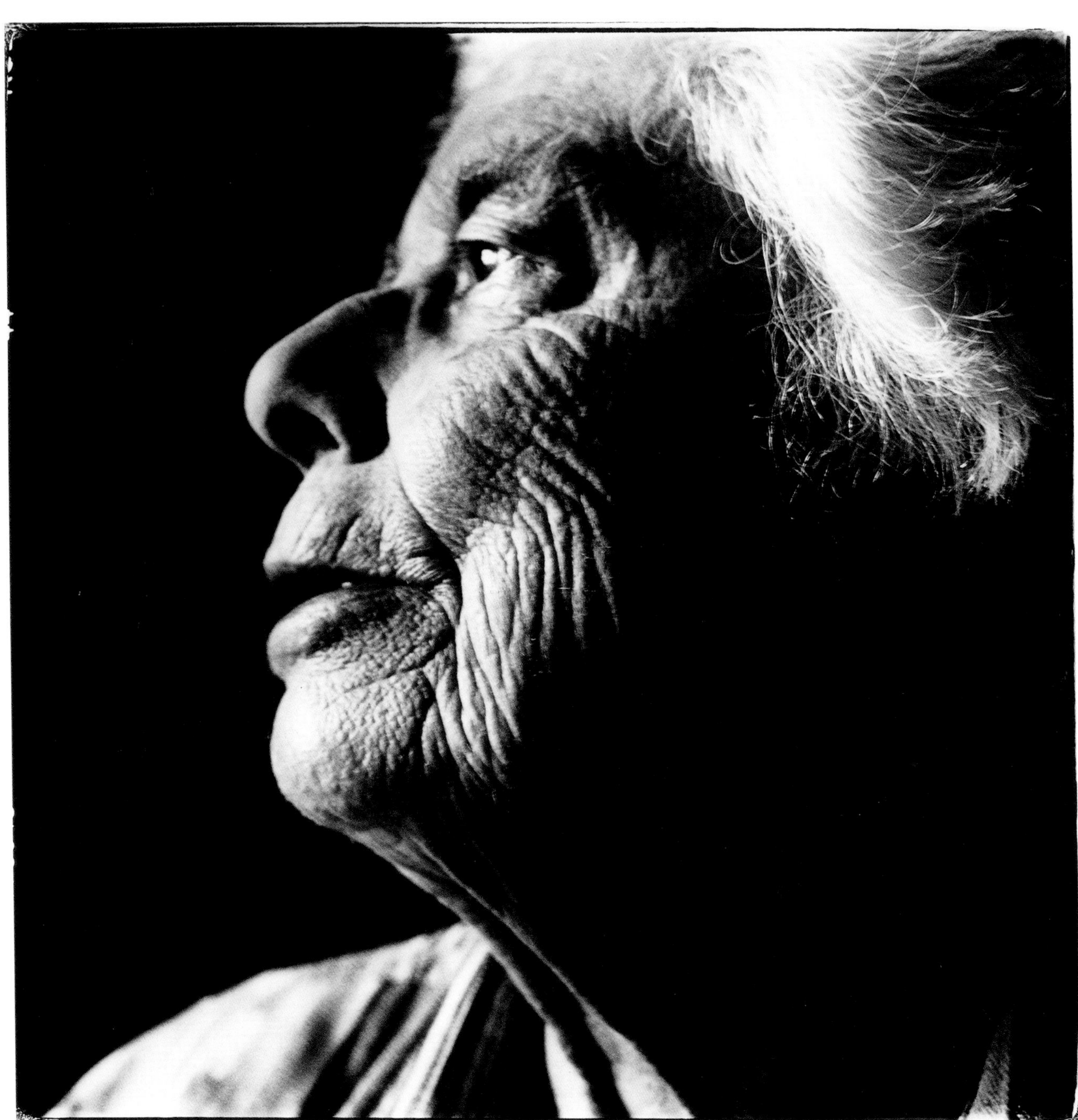

**Professor Phillipa Foot**

*Oxford, 23 August 1990*

"You ask a philosopher a question and after he or she has talked for a bit, you don't
understand your question any more."

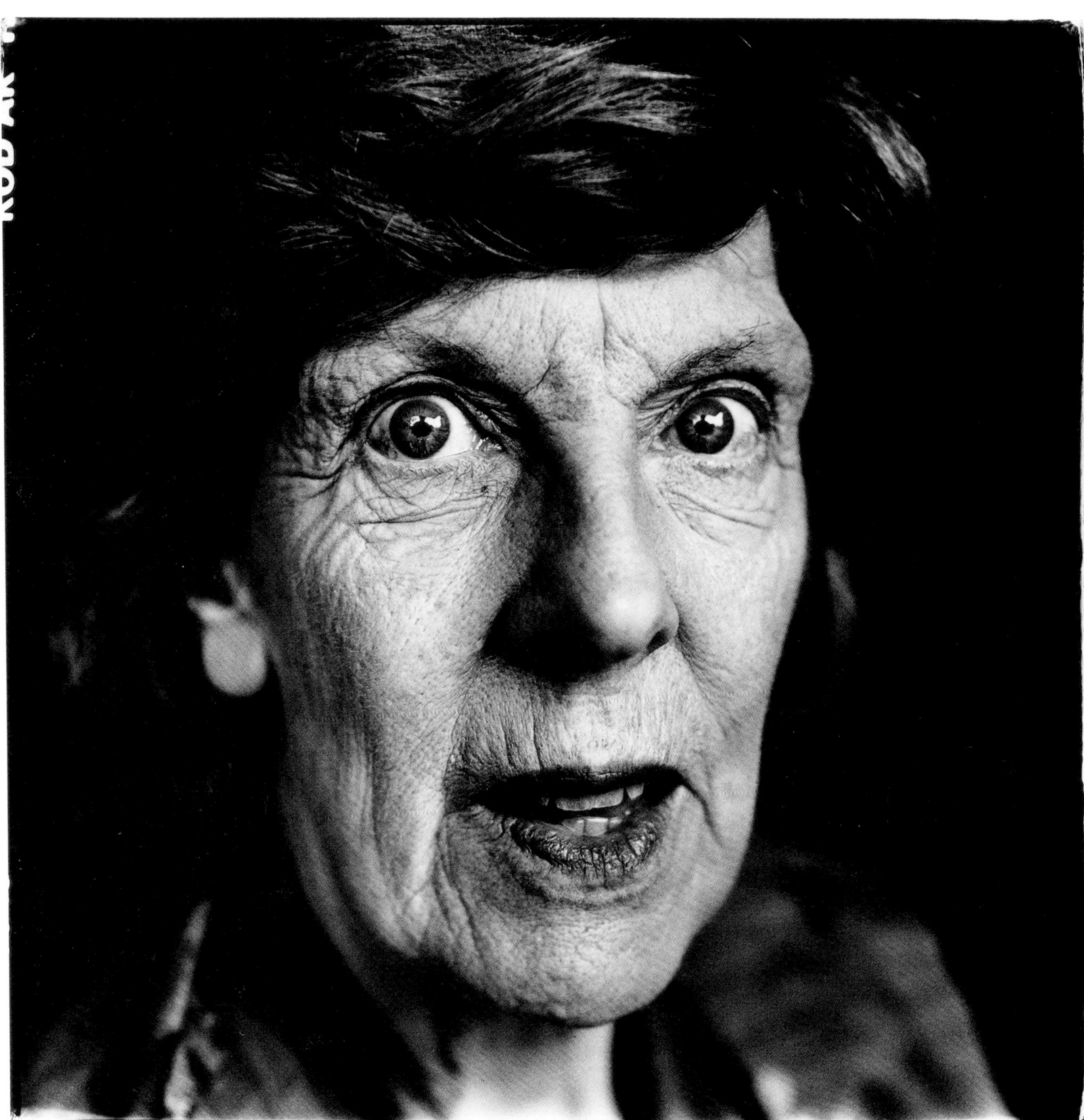

**Professor Michael Frede**

*Oxford, 28 February 1992*

"Philosophers cannot agree on anything. They certainly cannot agree on what philosophy actually is. Some people think that this is scandalous. When Lucius Gellius took up his position as Roman governor in Athens, he called the philosophers together and told them to put an end to their fruitless disputes and to come to some agreement. He generously offered his skills as an arbitrator (*Cicero, De leg. 1, 53*). Philosophers themselves again since Kant have found this situation scandalous. But I think there is much too much agreement, agreement for no good reason. I think it is wonderful that some people have the intellectual clarity, the insight, and the courage to show us that things can be seen quite differently. If one does not have this kind of clarity and strength oneself, one can always turn to history to get some distance from one's accustomed ways of thinking and to learn about alternatives."

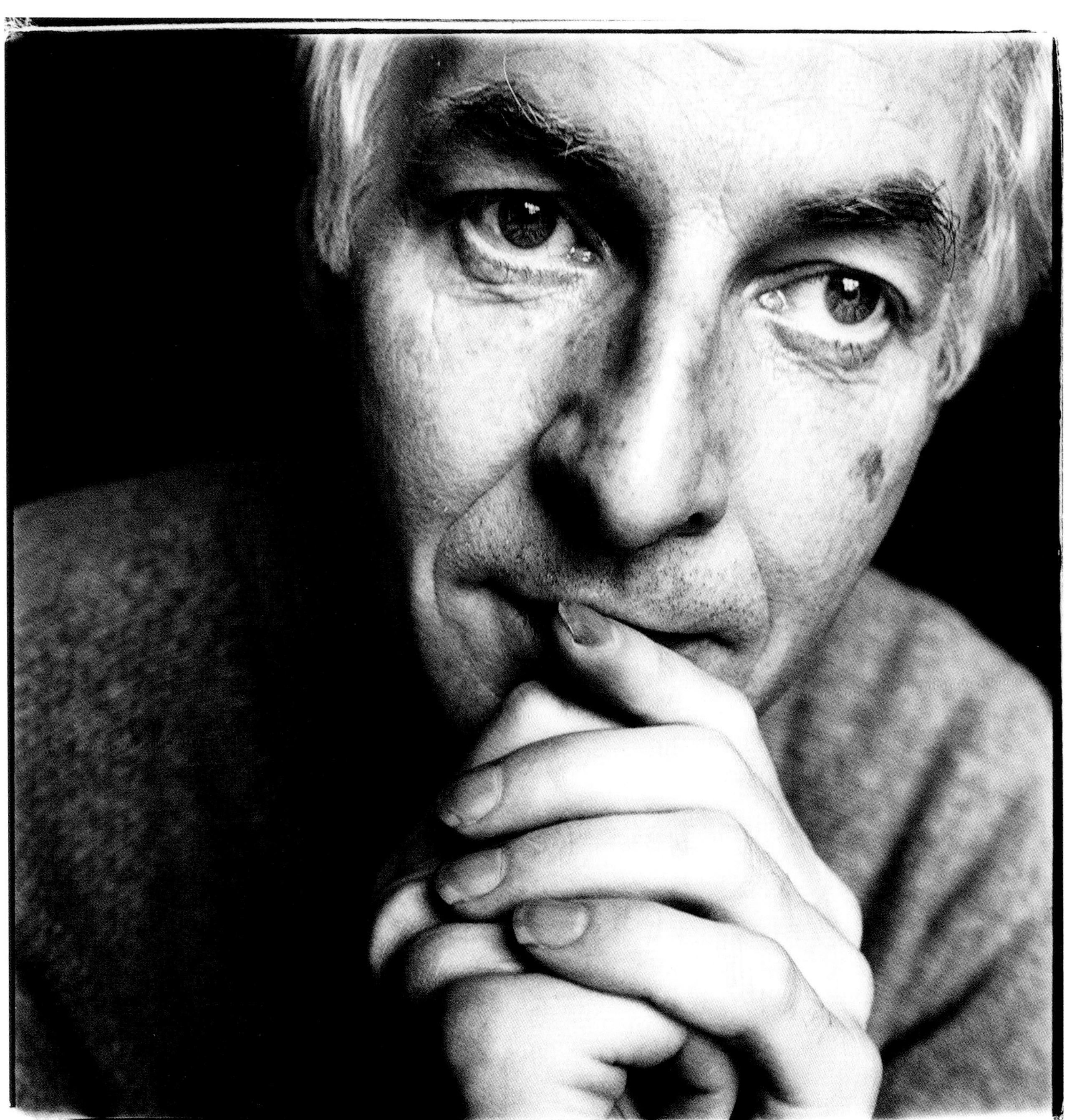

**Professor Dr Hans Georg Gadamer**

*Heidelberg, 5 November 1991*

"Philosophy is the way not to forget, that man is never God."

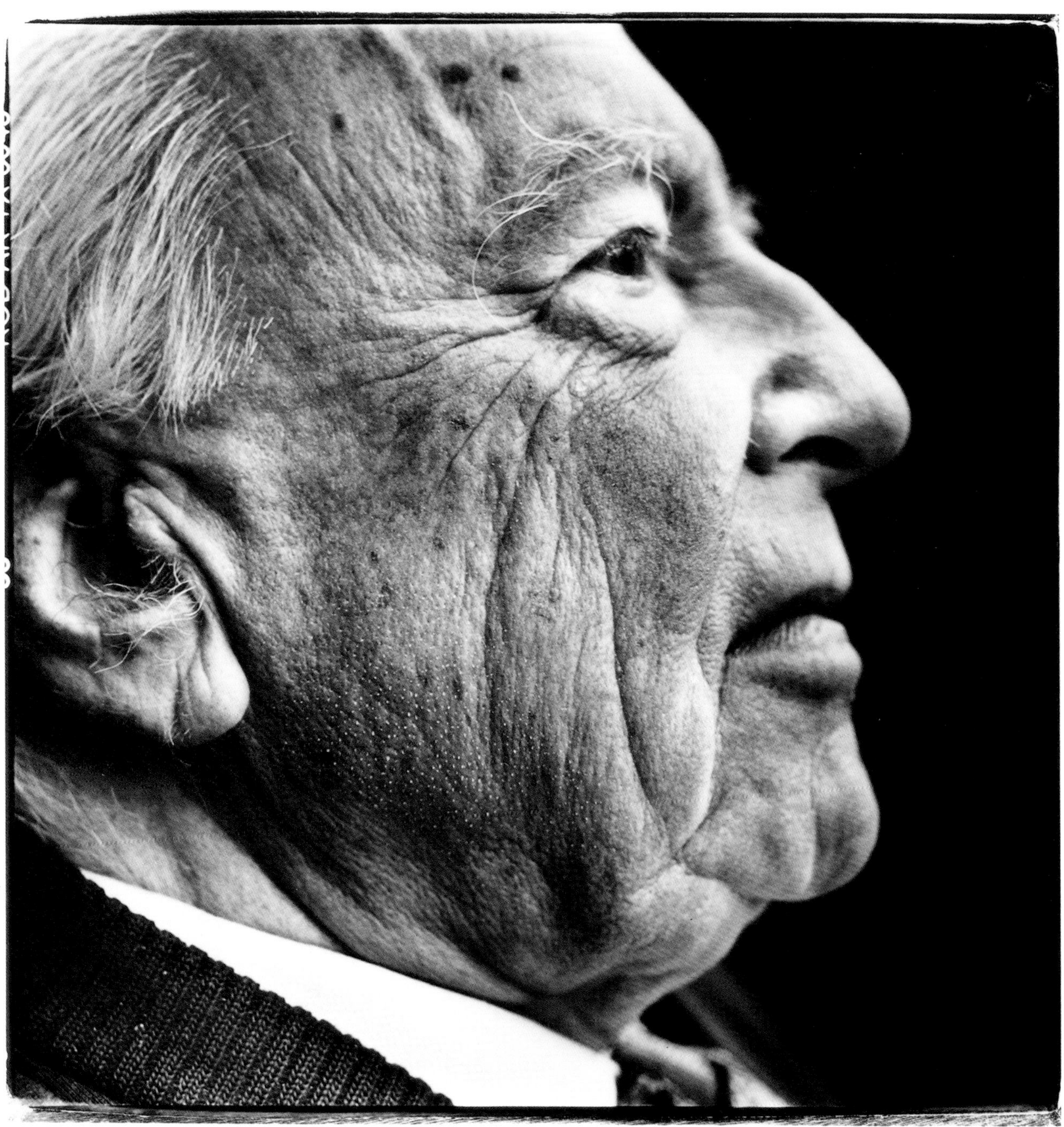

**Professor Peter Geach**

*Cambridge, 15 May 1990*

"I have been in love with logic ever since my father started me on logic in my teens. Logic of itself cannot give anyone the answer to any question of substance; but without logic we often do not know the import of what we know and often fall into fallacy and inconsistency."

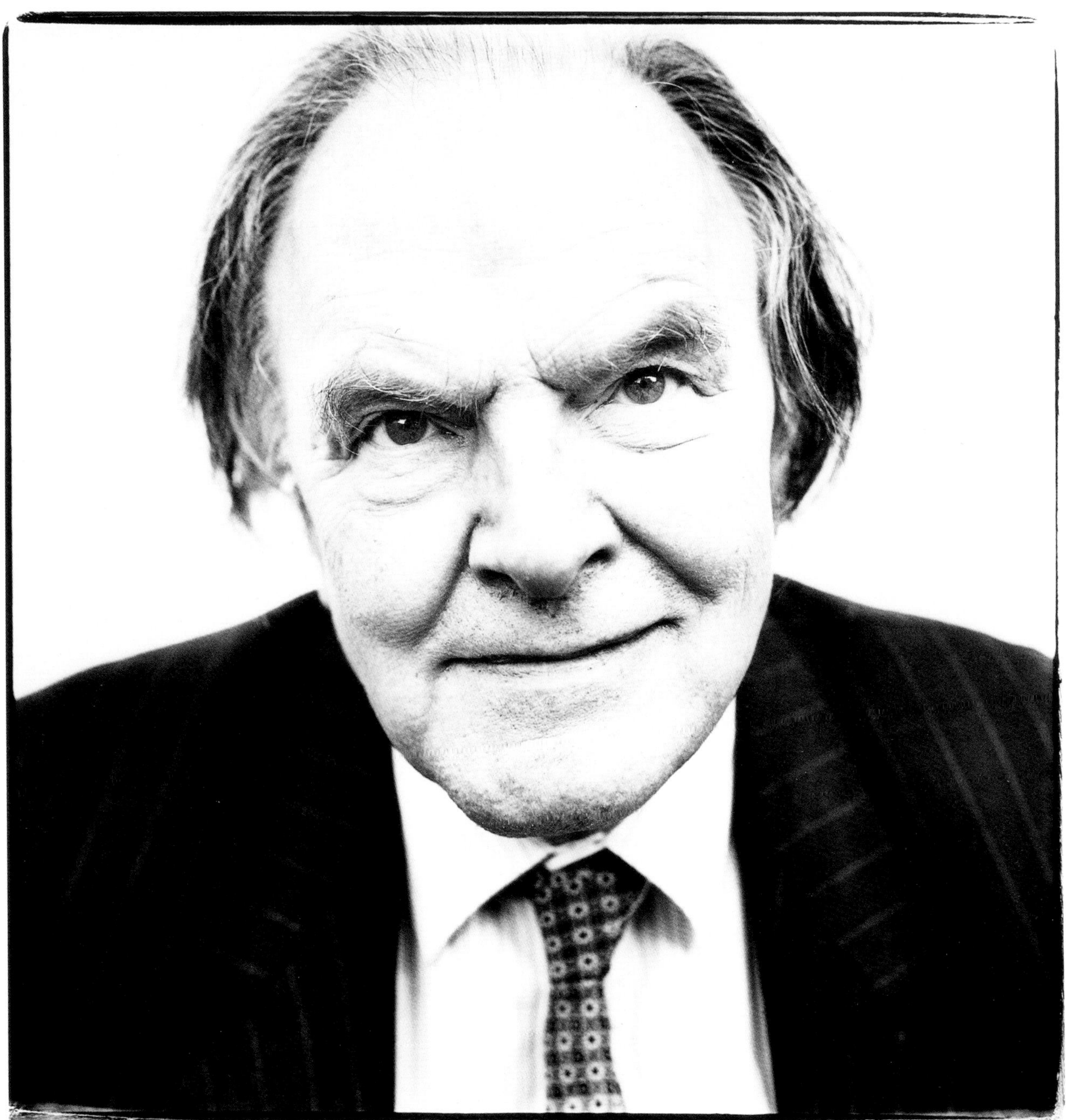

**Professor Margaret Gilbert**

*Oxford, 18 May, 1990*

Margaret Gilbert's philosophical work has centred on the human personality and social relations. Her book *On Social Facts* (1989) presents detailed accounts of shared action, social groups, group belief, and social convention. These help to show that, and how, group membership involves a deep constraining transformation of the individual.

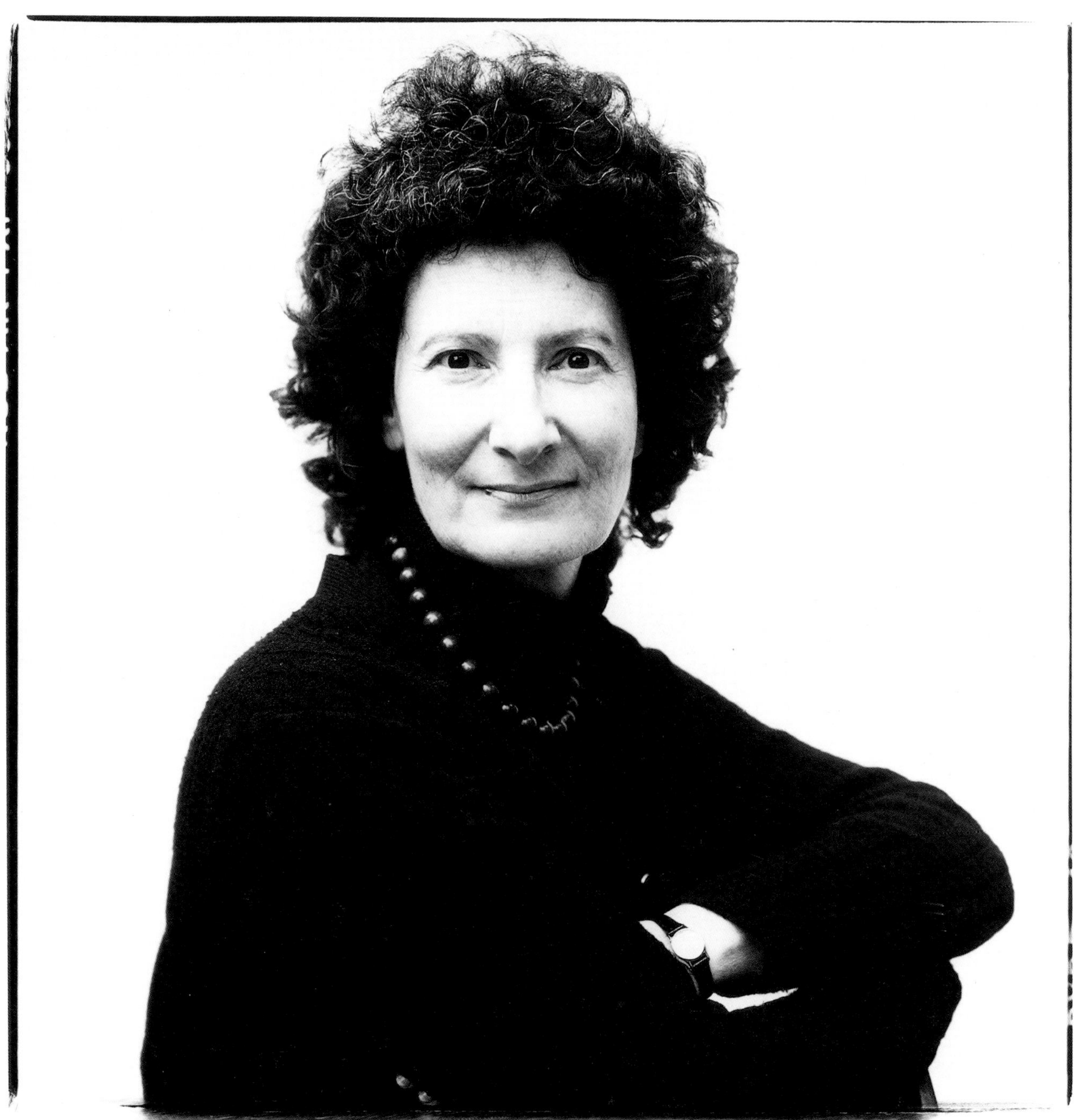

**Professor Dr Jürgen Habermas**

*Frankfurt, 6 November 1991*

"The future of the enlightenment, what might it consist in? We ought to succeed in showing how, within a predicament that is leaving ever narrower room for action, we are yet assuming responsibility for actions whose consequences are growing even longer and less easily surveyable. Moreover, we ought to be capable of showing this while at the same time being hesitant in the awareness of the danger that, as Benjamin knew, threatens even from the successes enjoyed in working together with a shared purpose."

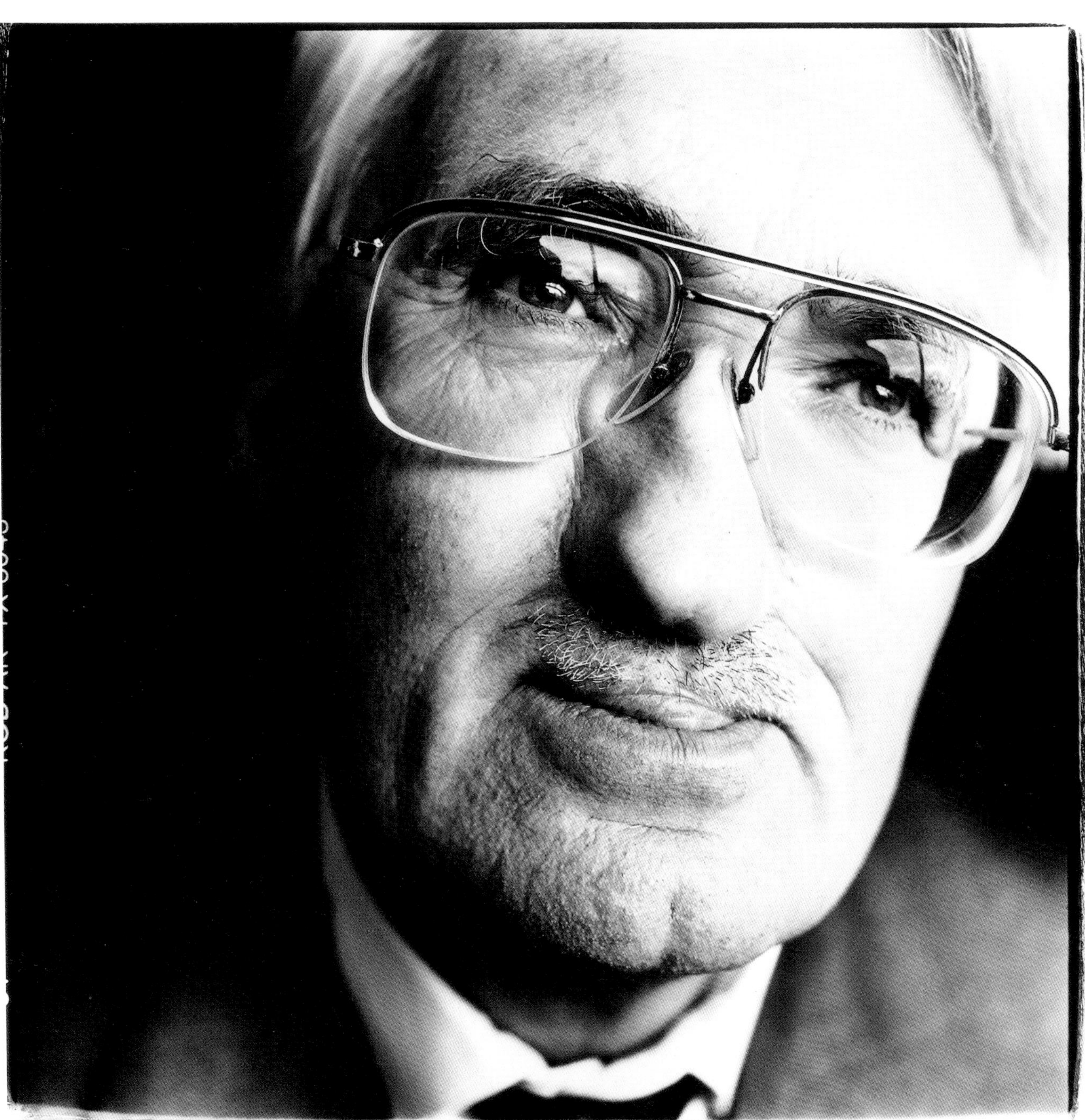

**Professor Sir Stuart Hampshire**

*Oxford, 5 July 1990*

"Truth, Existence, Knowledge, Causality, Identity, Goodness: these are the principal notions which philosophers examine. Intelligent persons normally have thoughtful and useful lives without pausing to look into these notions and into the connections between them. Once one starts to look into them, it is difficult to stop. The looking becomes part of life, and in some cases a large part."

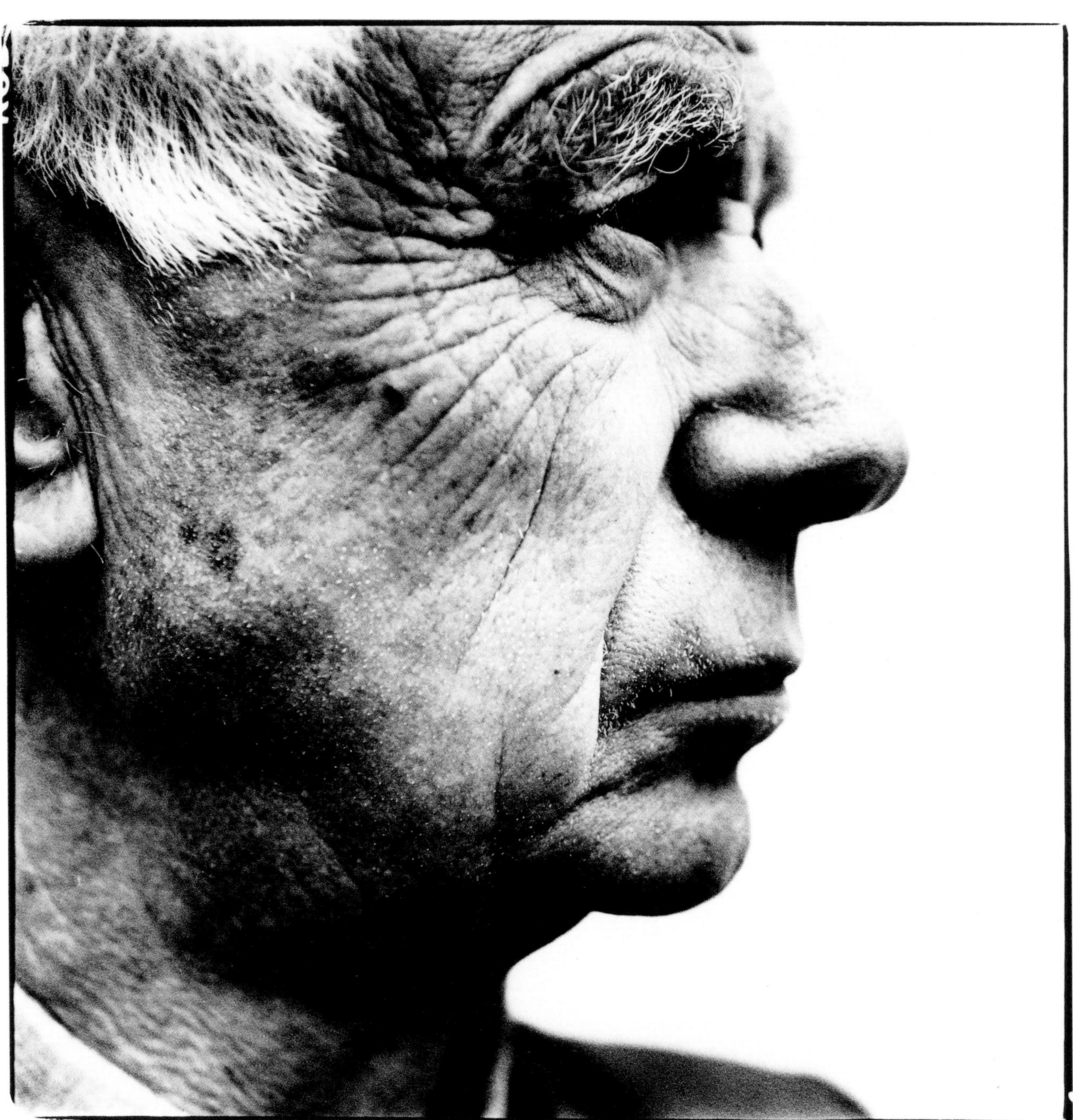

**Professor R M Hare**

*Oxford, 9 May 1990*

Richard Hare, moral philosopher, has made substantial contributions to ethical theory and its application to practical moral issues. His aim has been to establish moral thinking as a rational and relevant activity, by showing that moral precepts, although quite different in their status and function from statements of scientific fact, can nevertheless be the conclusions of rational thought, to which all must in reason assent. His theory combines elements drawn from Kant and the utilitarians, usually thought of as irreconcilable.

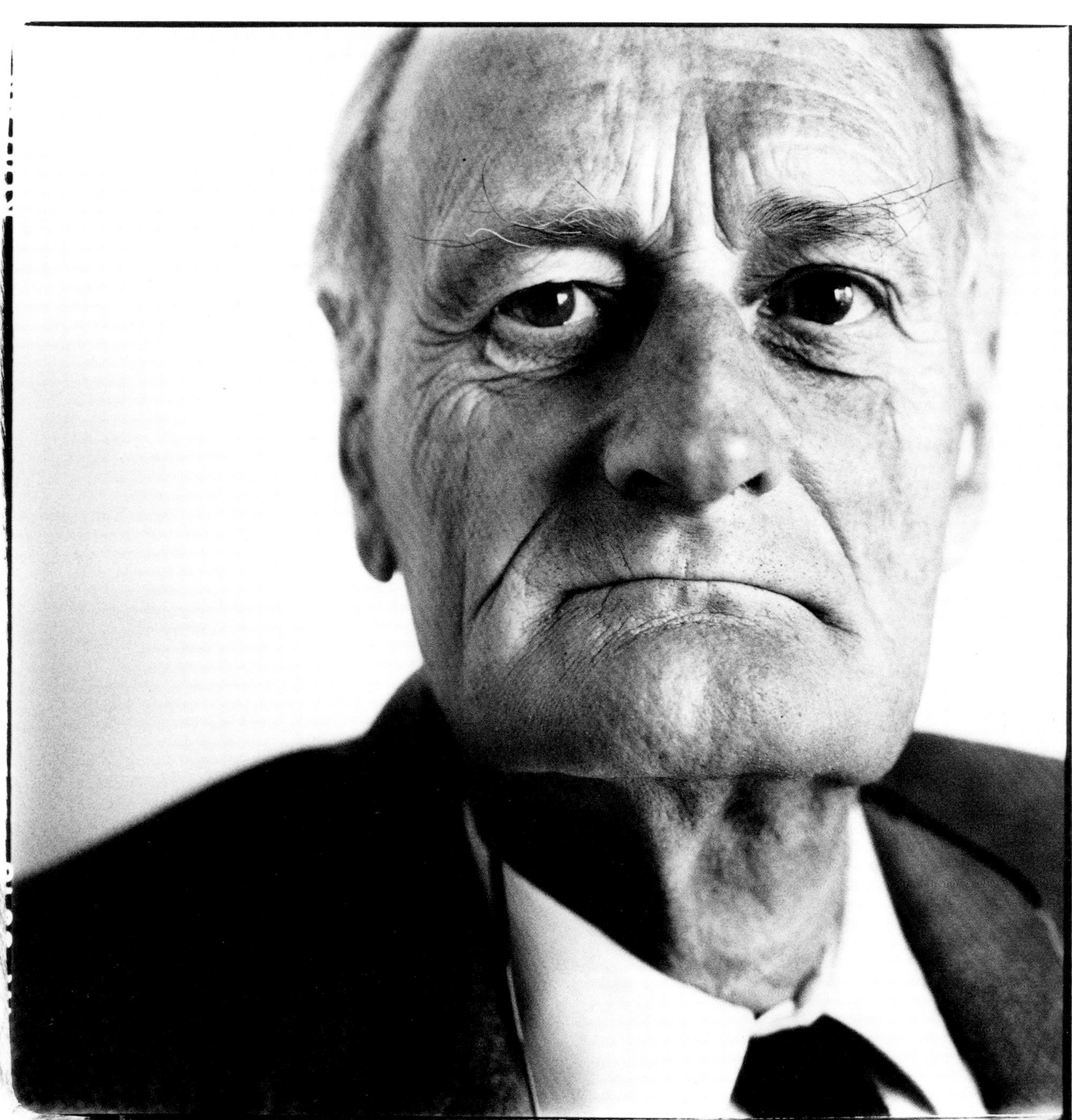

**Professor H L A Hart**

*Oxford, 5 July 1990*

"To be frank I think the idea of a 50-100 word summary is an absurd idea … I advise you to drop it."

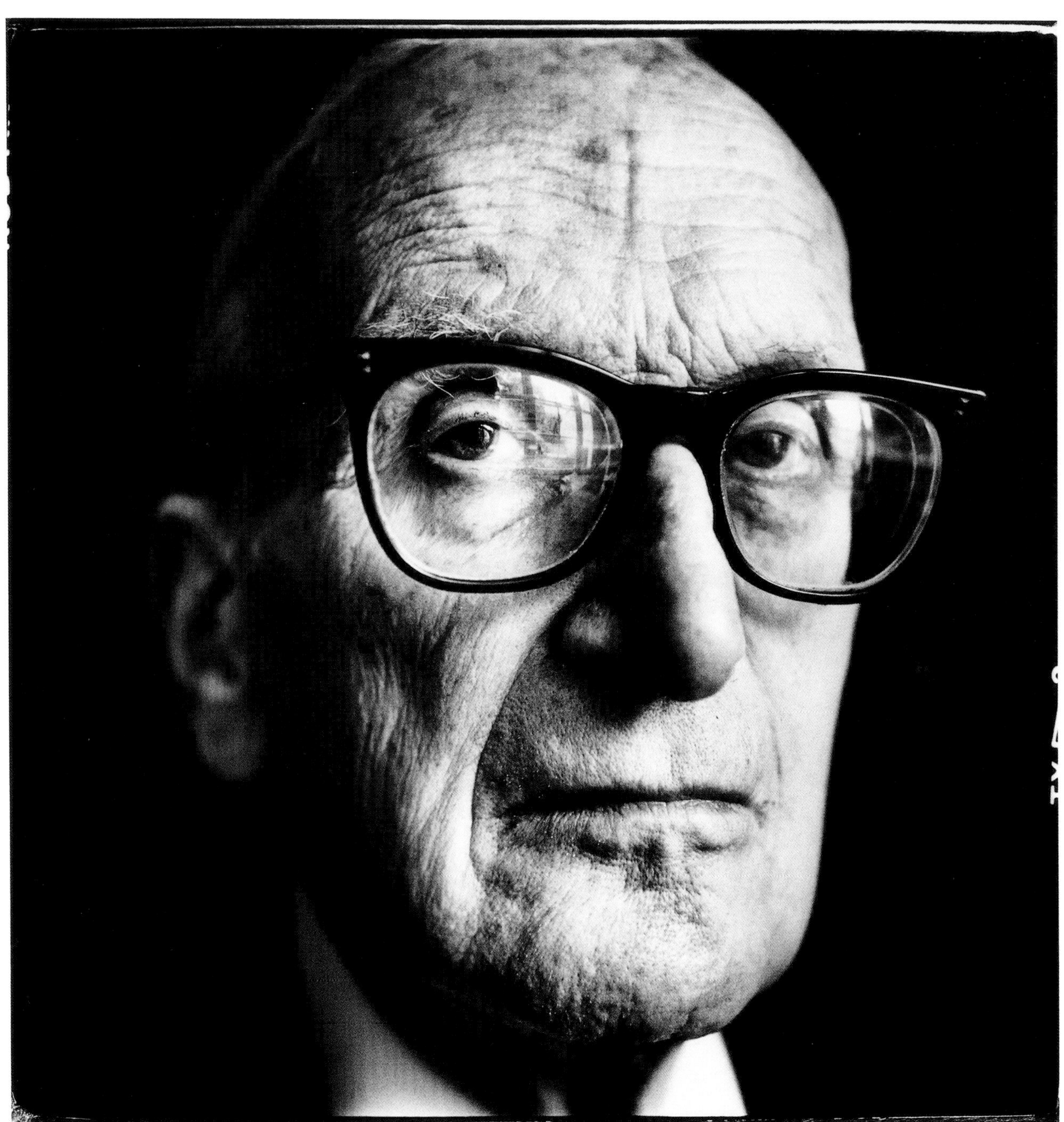

**Dr Jane Heal**

*Cambridge, 18 March 1993*

"Philosophy is in the business of articulating as clearly as possible what can be said on fundamental questions about knowledge, value and existence and of asking whether and how views on these issues can be defended. Carrying forward this discussion, with as much imagination and integrity as we can muster, is a central strand in a self-aware, humane and tolerant culture and it is to this that I would like to regard myself as contributing."

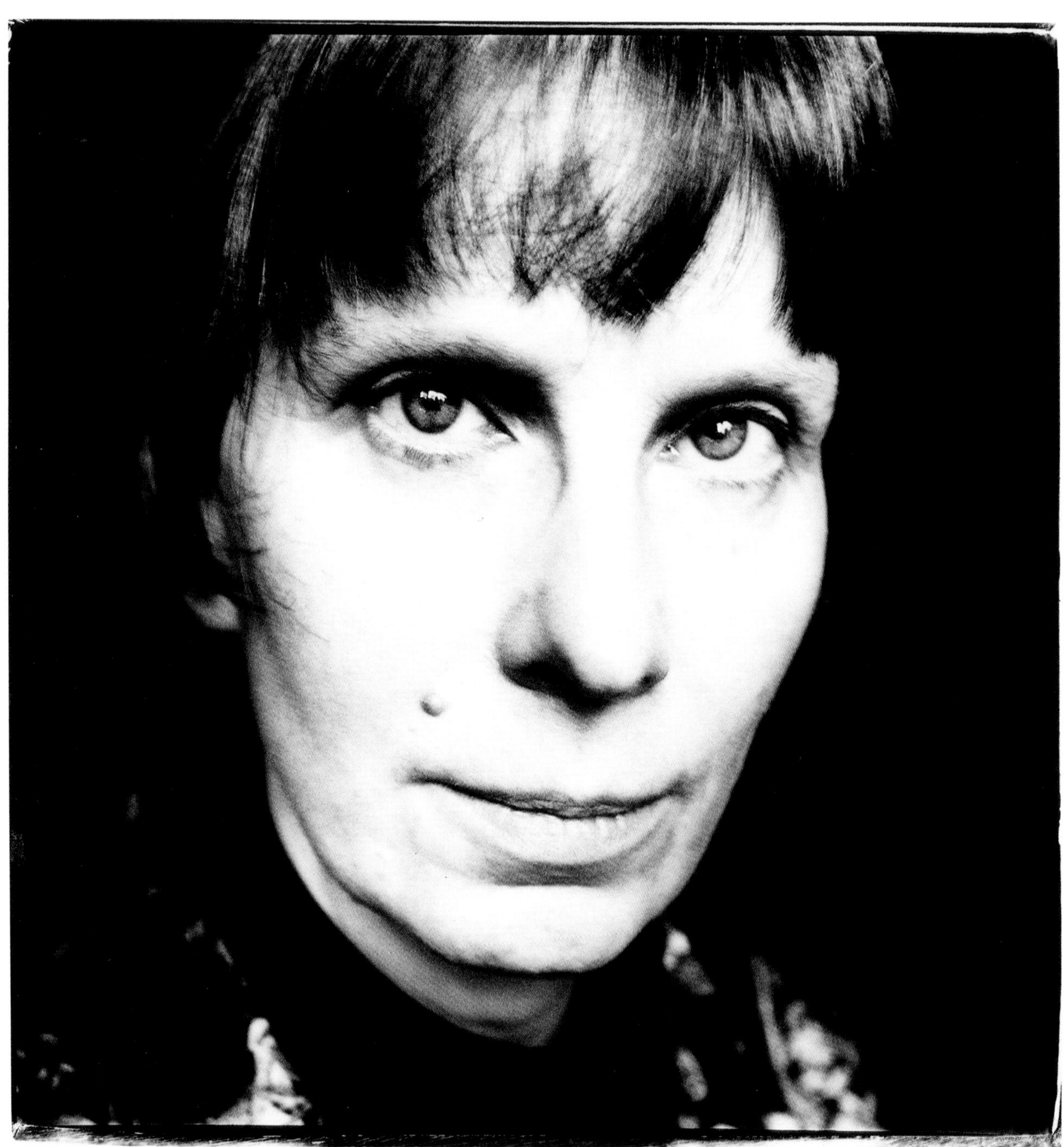

**Professor Carl Gustave Hempel**

*Princeton, 26 May 1990*

"It is a rather widely held opinion that history, in contradistinction to the so-called physical sciences, is concerned with the description of particular events of the past rather than with the search for general laws which might govern those events. As a characterization of the type of problem in which some historians are mainly interested, this view probably can not be denied; as a statement of the theoretical function of general laws in scientific historical research, it is certainly unacceptable."

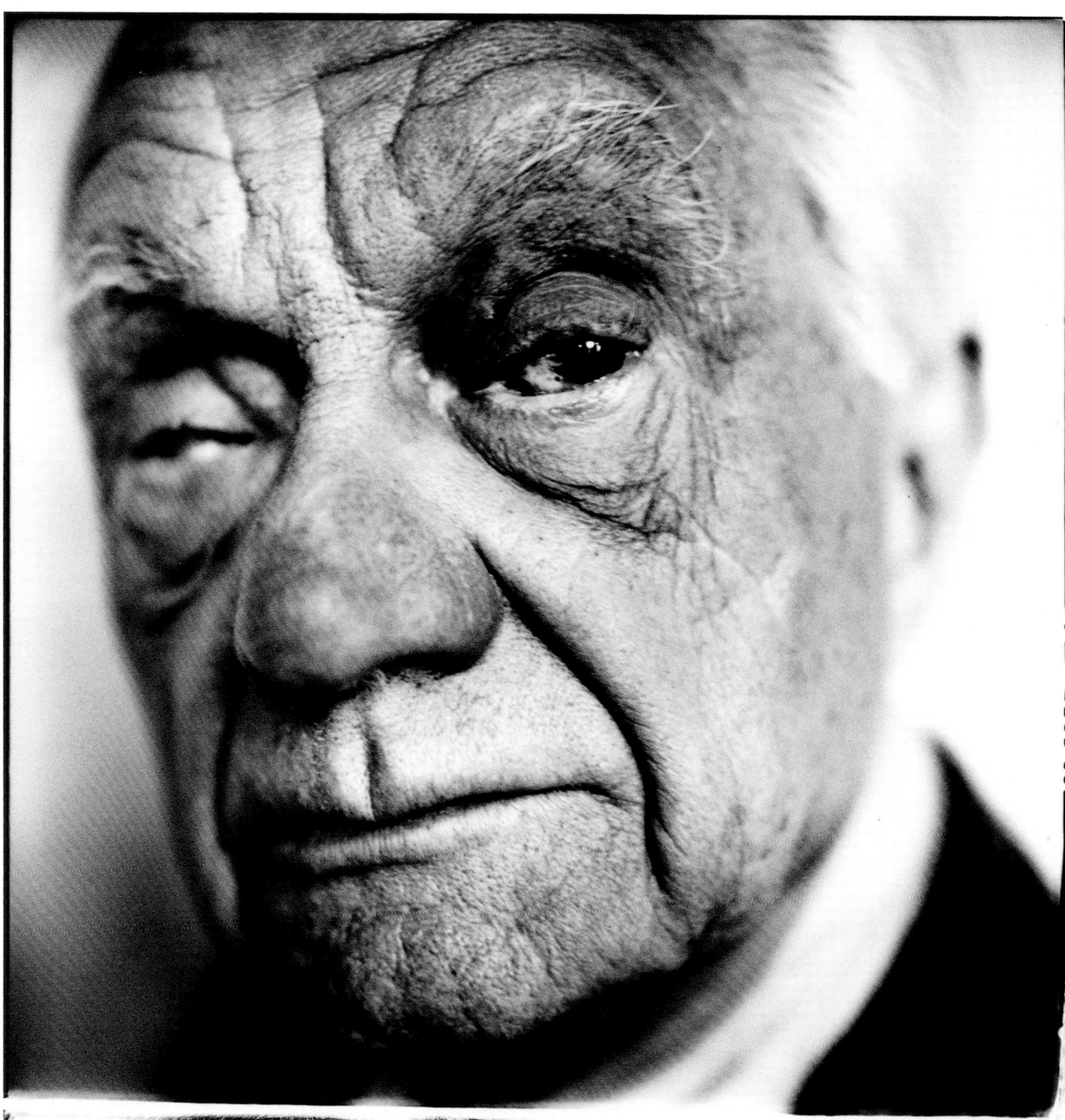

**Professor Martin Hollis**

*Norwich, 15 May 1990*

"The social sciences are not just labourers, nor philosophy just an under-labourer, in the attempt to discover the truth about Adam. They also put ideas into Adam's head. Some of these ideas strengthen his power to be his own sovereign artificer. Others distance him perilously from his handiwork. But at least they have helped him to see better what is in the world, by showing him his own activity." *Conclusion to 'The Cunning of Reason'*

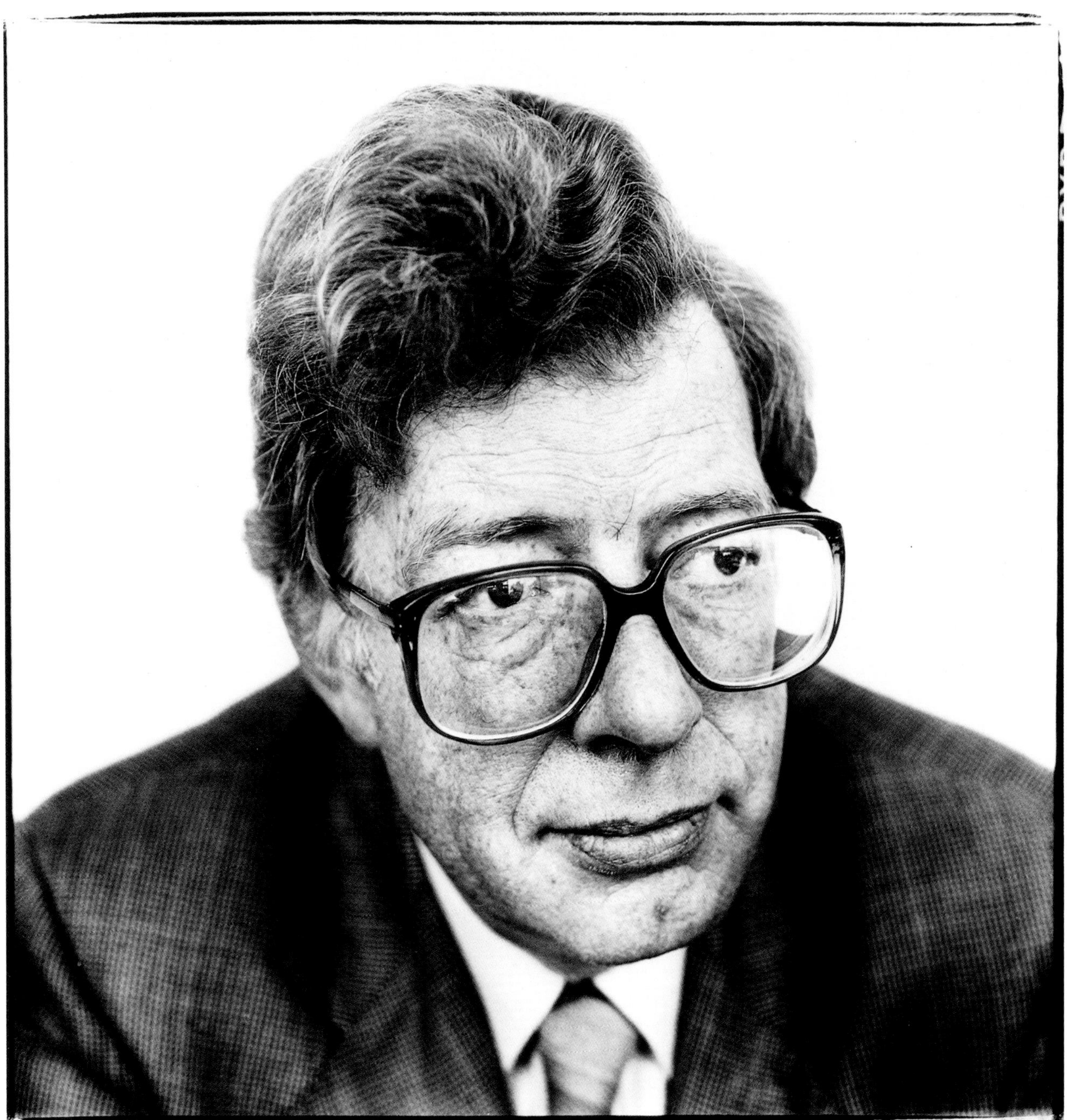

**Professor Ted Honderich**

*London, 13 February 1990*

"Ted Honderich is Grote Professor of the Philosophy of Mind and Logic at University College London, and his principal book is *A Theory of Determinism: The Mind, Neuroscience, and Life-Hopes*. It includes accounts of the relation of the mind to the brain, the origins of such mental events as choosing and believing, and of the nature of action. It also provides a resolution of the ancient but persistent problem of Freewill. Two of his interests in political philosophy are represented by books on political violence and Conservatism. He has also published a book about attempted justifications of punishment by the State. He is now writing a book in the Philosophy of Mind, on the nature of experience. He is a committed cyclist."

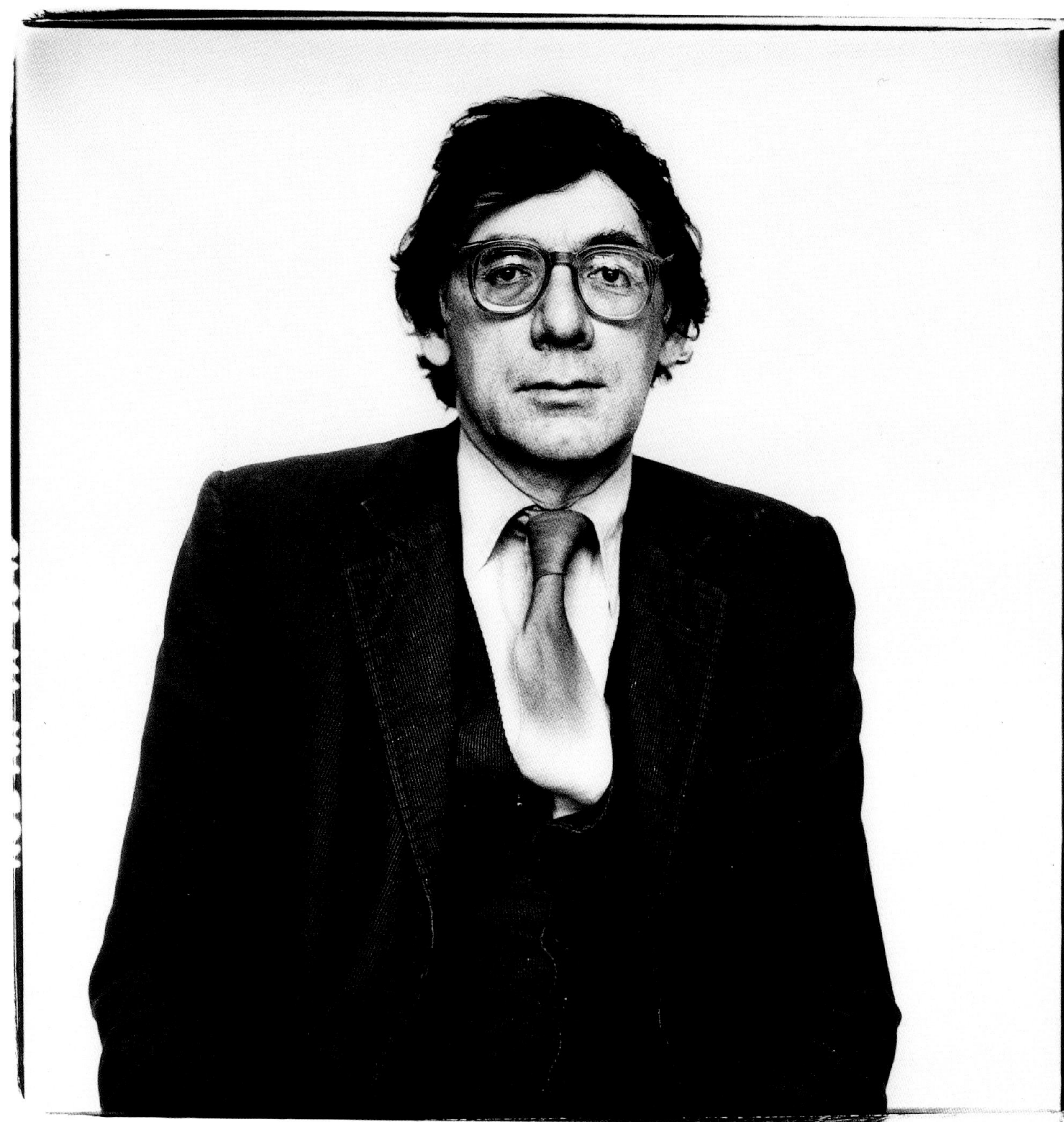

**Professor Susan Hurley**

*Oxford, 7 June 1990*

"Susan Hurley's work revives a classical idea about rationality in a modern framework, by developing analogies between the structure of personality and the structure of society in the context of contemporary work in philosophy of mind, ethics, decision theory and social choice theory."

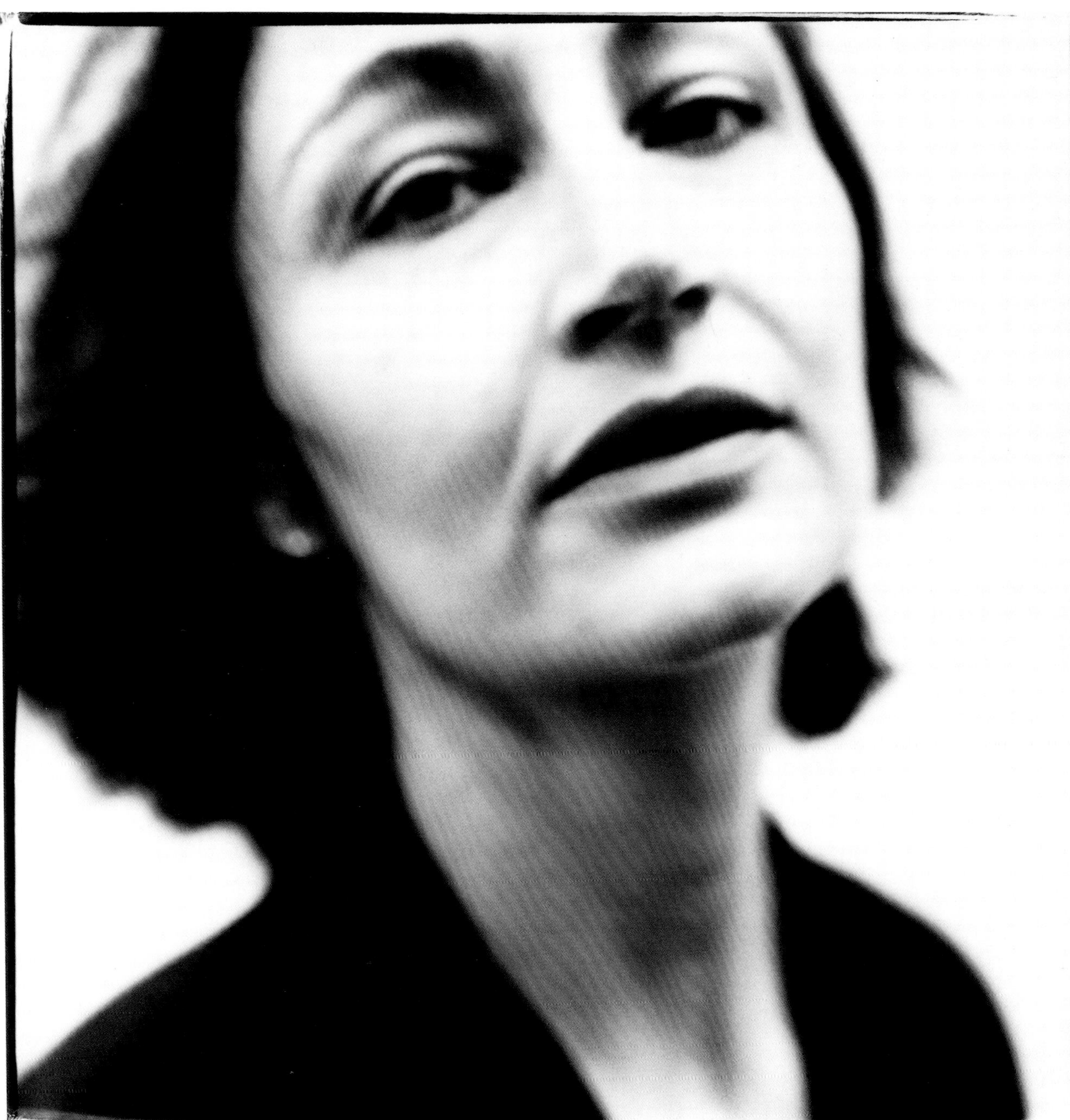

**Professor Hide Ishiguro**

*London, 8 August 1990*

"Philosophy, is something that those involved with can identify, without being able to agree on how to characterize it. I would describe it as the activity of attempting to understand basic concepts, concepts that we use when we try to grasp our relation with reality and think of possibilities. Because of its abstract subject matter, philosophy fails completely if it is not carried out with a sturdy sense of reality. Since the world is so amorphous, philosophy is an activity which demands a feel for rigour and open-mindness at the same time."

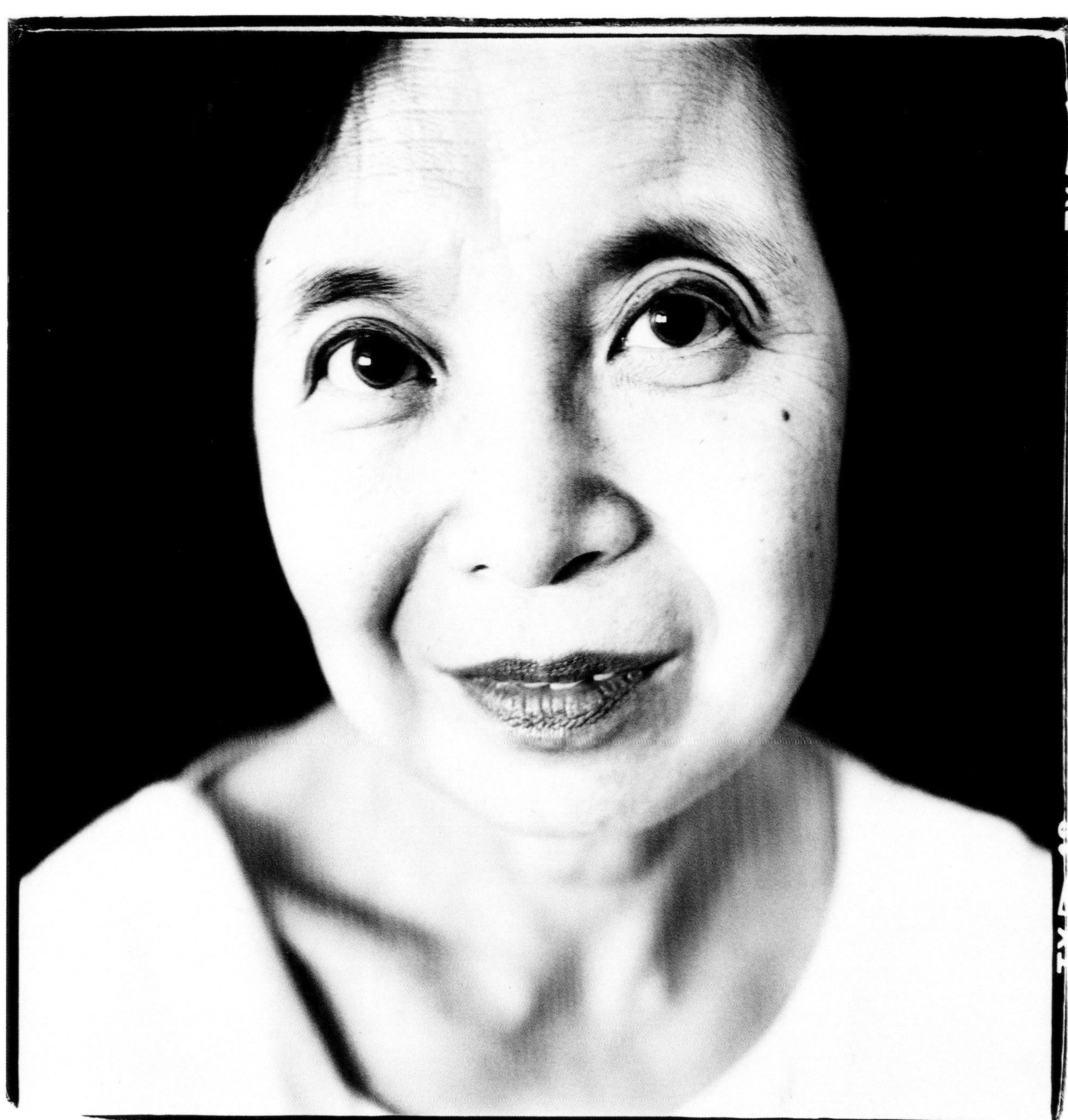

**C L R James**

*London, 26 April 1989*

"Time would pass, old empires would fall and new ones take their place, the relations of countries and the relations of classes had to change, before I discovered that it is not quality of goods and utility which matter, but movement; not where or what you have, but where you have come from, where you are going and the rate at which you are getting there."

*'Beyond a Boundary', Chapter 8*

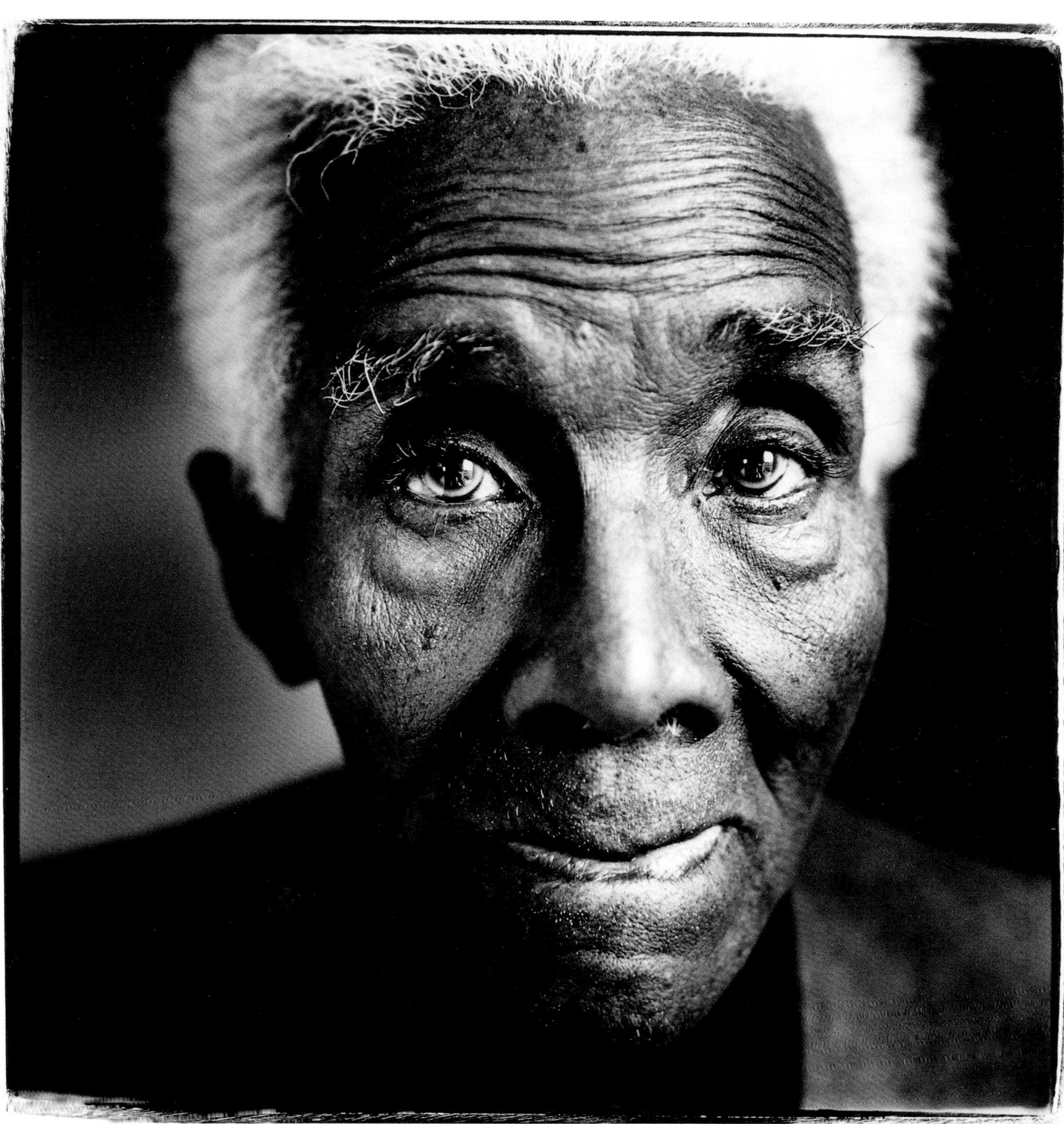

**Professor Frank Jackson**

*Princeton, 26 May 1990*

''Science tells us a lot about the world and a lot about ourselves. We also have our own ideas
on both subjects – ideas which predate modern science and which derive from our
acquaintance with the world and with ourselves. The challenge is to understand how these two
pictures of the world and these two pictures of ourselves are related, and to do so without
denying the reality and importance of either picture. The specialists in the various departments
of knowledge know most about their subject matters. The philosopher seeks to make sense of
the overall picture."

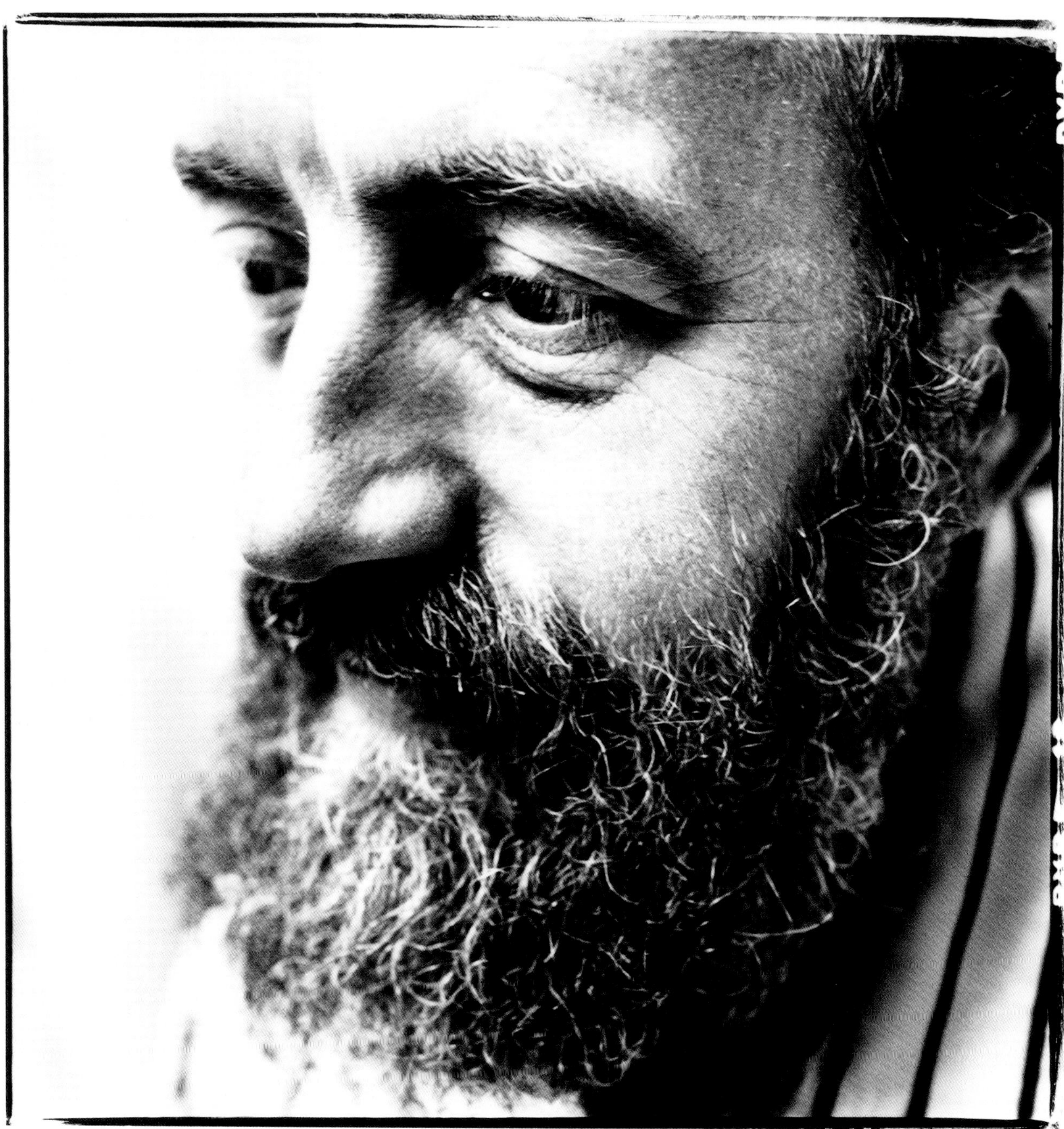

**Professor Richard Kearney**

*Union Hall Eire, 27 December 1990*

"Philosophy keeps us on our toes by keeping our minds open – open to questioning ourselves and others. It begins with a mixture of unease (that we are not fully at one with the world) and wonder (that the world exists at all). I myself have tried to explore a philosophy of **imagination** as root of human recollection and transcendence, as an inexhaustible power to open up possible worlds of meaning."

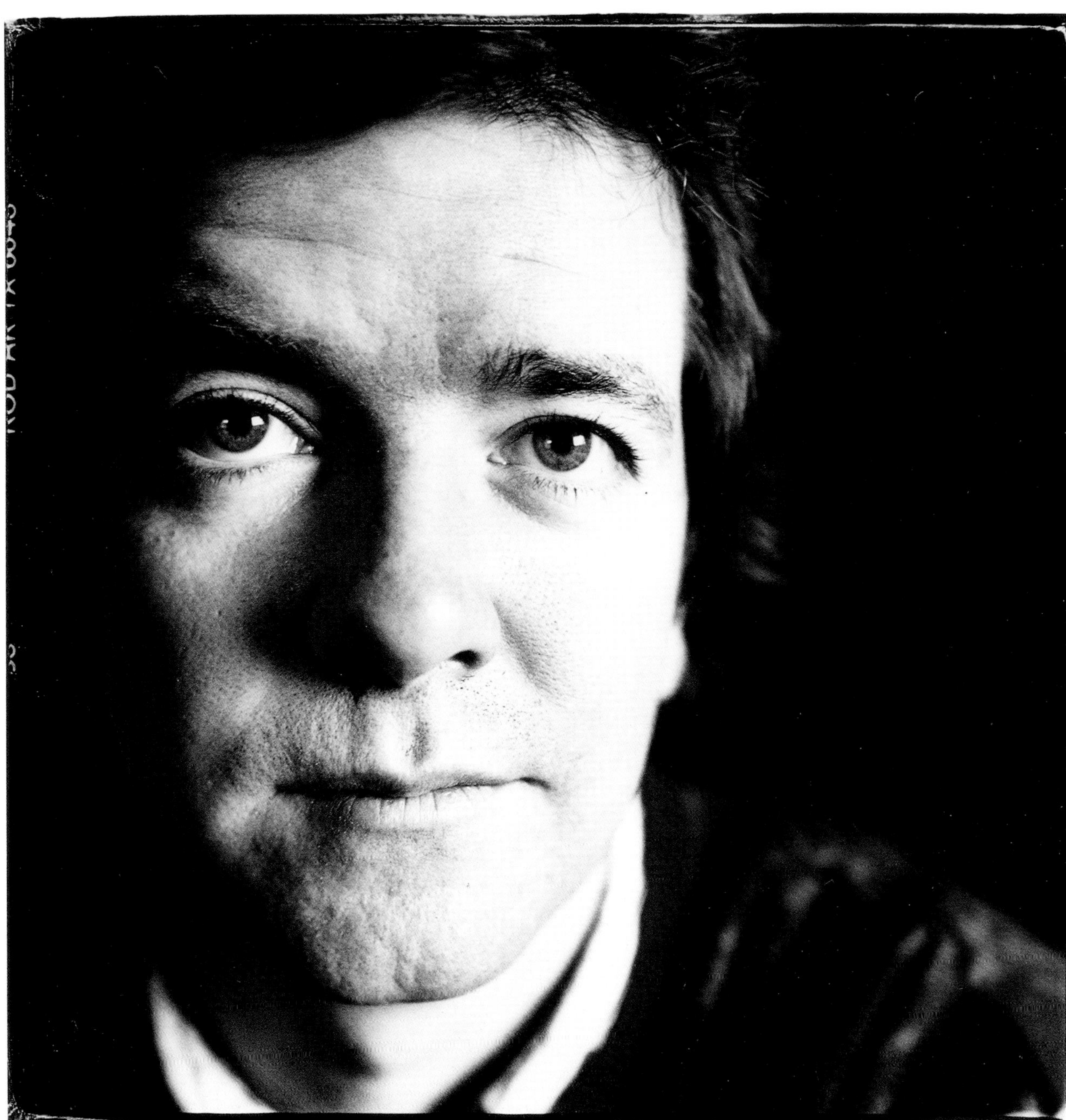

**Sir Anthony Kenny**

*Oxford, 28 February 1992*

"Philosophy is an unusual, indeed unique discipline. Some people would claim that it was the most attractive of all disciplines, for the following reason. On the one hand philosophy seems to resemble a science in that the philosopher, like the scientist, is in pursuit of truth. In philosophy, as in science, there are discoveries made. There are certain things which philosophers of the present day understand which even the greatest philosophers of earlier generations failed to understand. The philosopher, therefore, has the excitement of belonging to a continuing, cooperative, cumulative endeavour, in the way that a scientist does. Each practitioner may nourish the hope of adding a stone to the cairn: one may make one's tiny contribution to the building of the great edifice. And thus philosophy has some of the attractions of the natural sciences.

On the other hand, philosophy seems to have the attraction of the arts and of the humanistic disciplines, in the following way. Unlike works of science, classic works of philosophy do not date. If we want to learn physics or chemistry, as opposed to their history, we do not nowadays read Newton or Faraday. Matters are different in the case of literature: when we read Homer and Shakespeare it is not merely in order to learn about the quaint things that passed through people's minds in those far off days. The same seems to be true of philosophy. We read Plato and Aristotle not simply in a spirit of antiquarian curiosity, but because we want to share their philosophical insights. Philosophy, then, seems uniquely attractive in that it combines being a discipline in pursuit of truth in which, as in science, discoveries are made, with being, like literature, a humane discipline in which great works do not become obsolete with age."

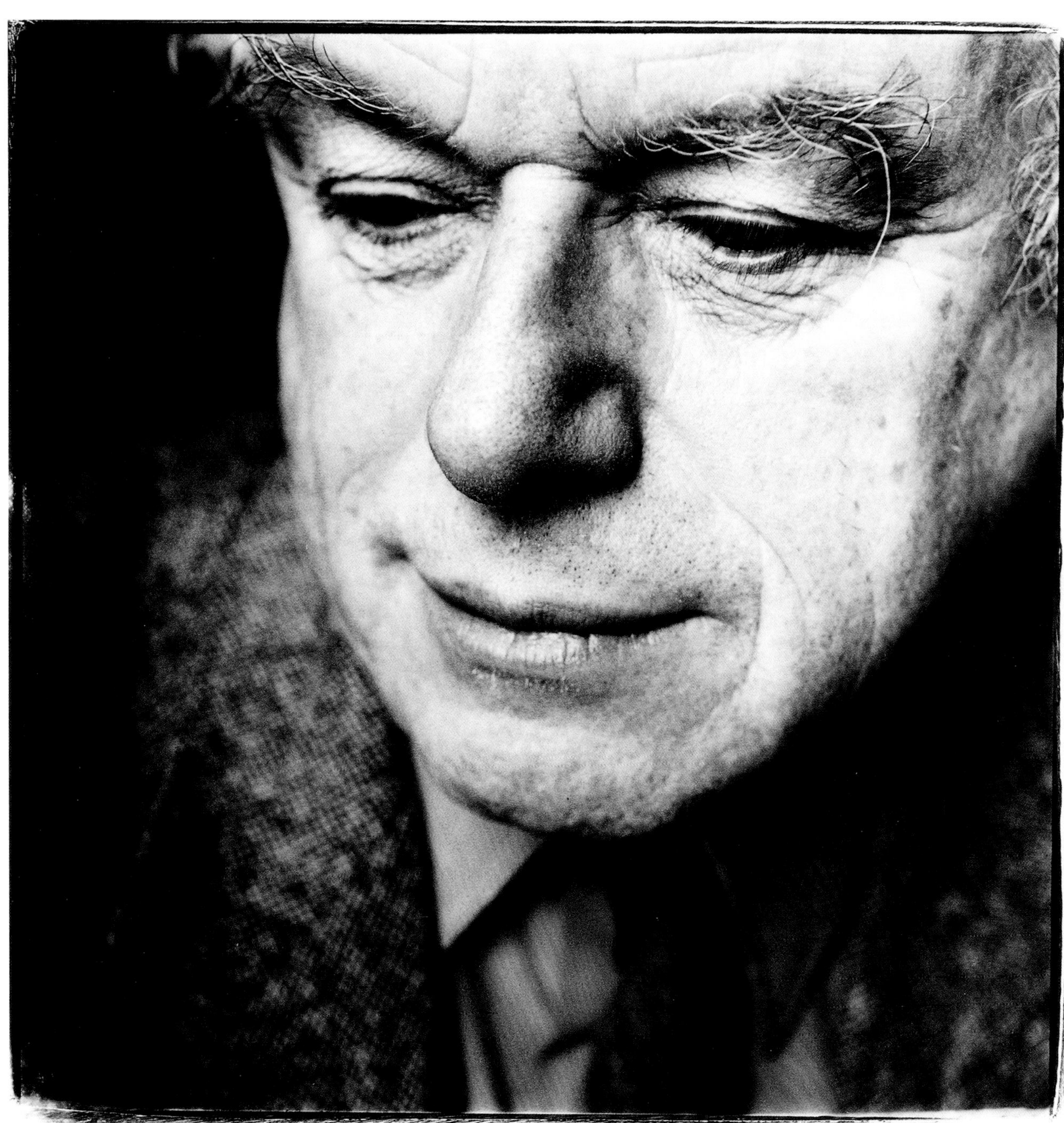

**Dr Leszek Kolakowski**

*Oxford, 17 August 1992*

"And is it not a plausible suspicion that if 'to be' were pointless and the universe void of
meaning, we would never have achieved not only the ability to imagine otherwise but even the
ability to think precisely this: that 'to be' is indeed pointless and the universe void of meaning?"

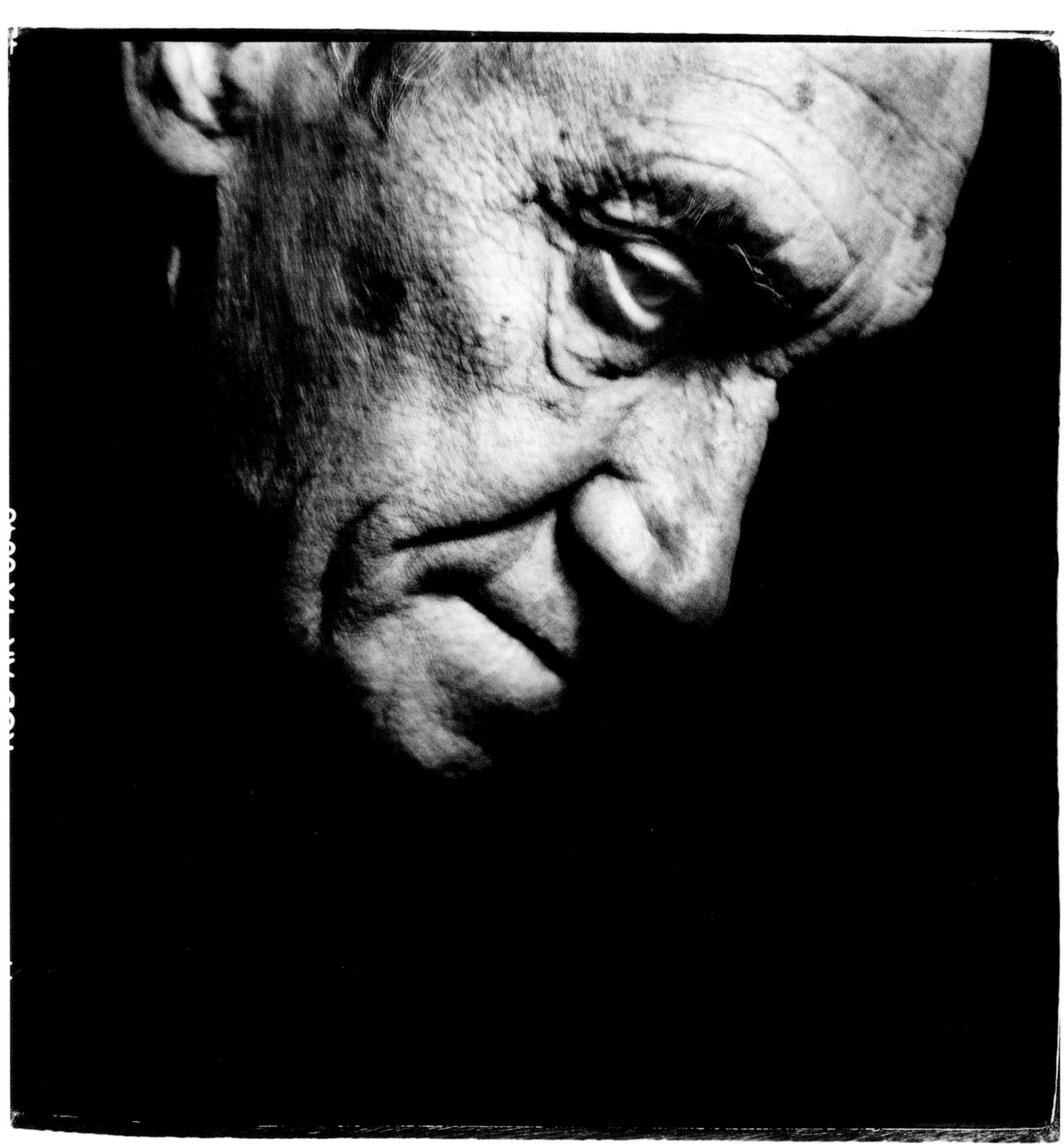

**Professor Saul Kripke**

*Oxford, 18 May 1990*

"I have been interested in philosophy since about the age of 12 or 13 when the question how I ever knew that I wasn't dreaming, led me to look at Descartes. I have been hooked on the subject ever since.

My work has included analytical metaphysics, the philosophy of language, epistemology and logic. I have also done some work of a technical or mathematical character, and have written on the later philosophy of Wittgenstein."

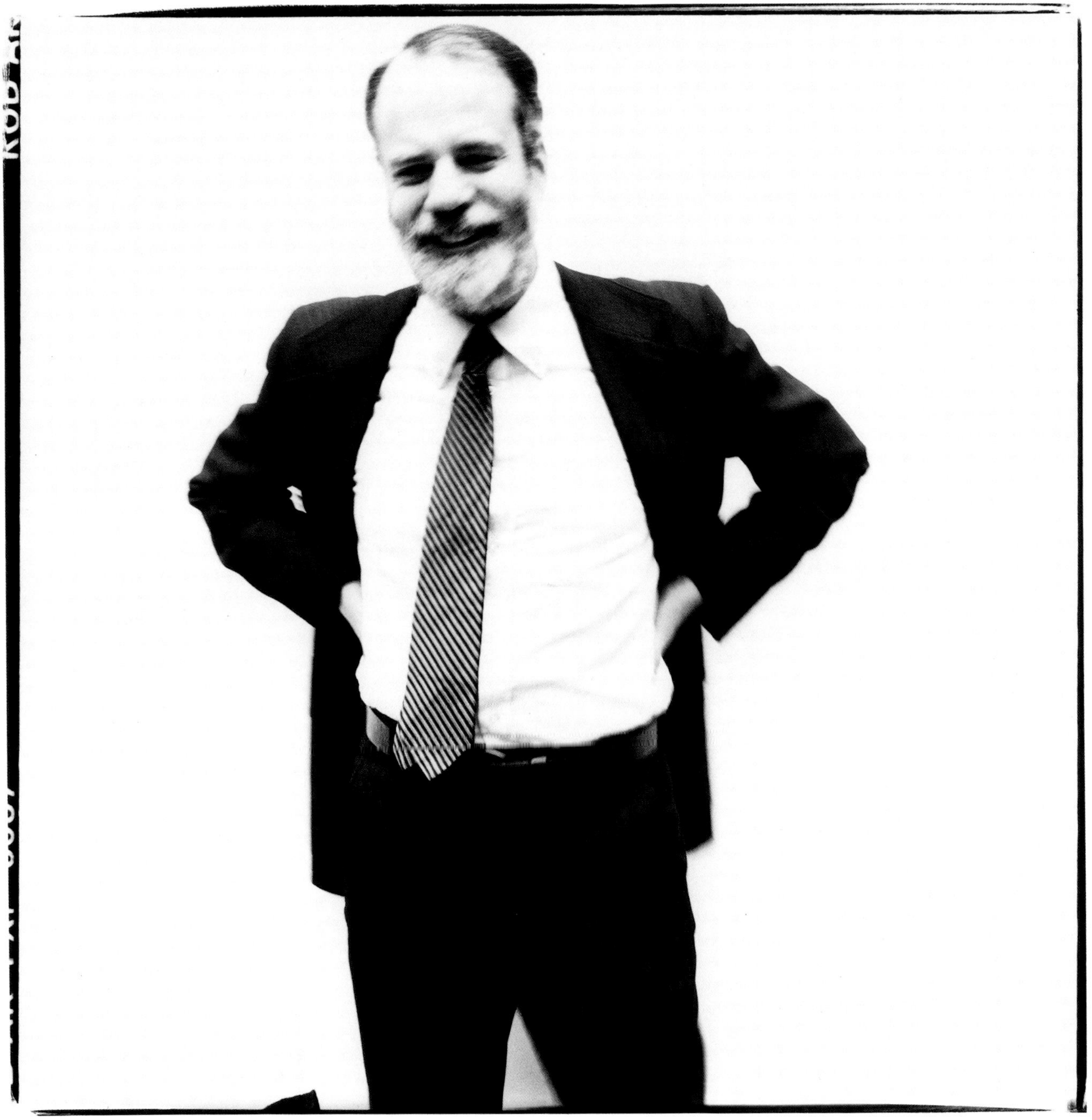

**Professor Raymond Klibansky**

*Oxford, 17 August 1992*

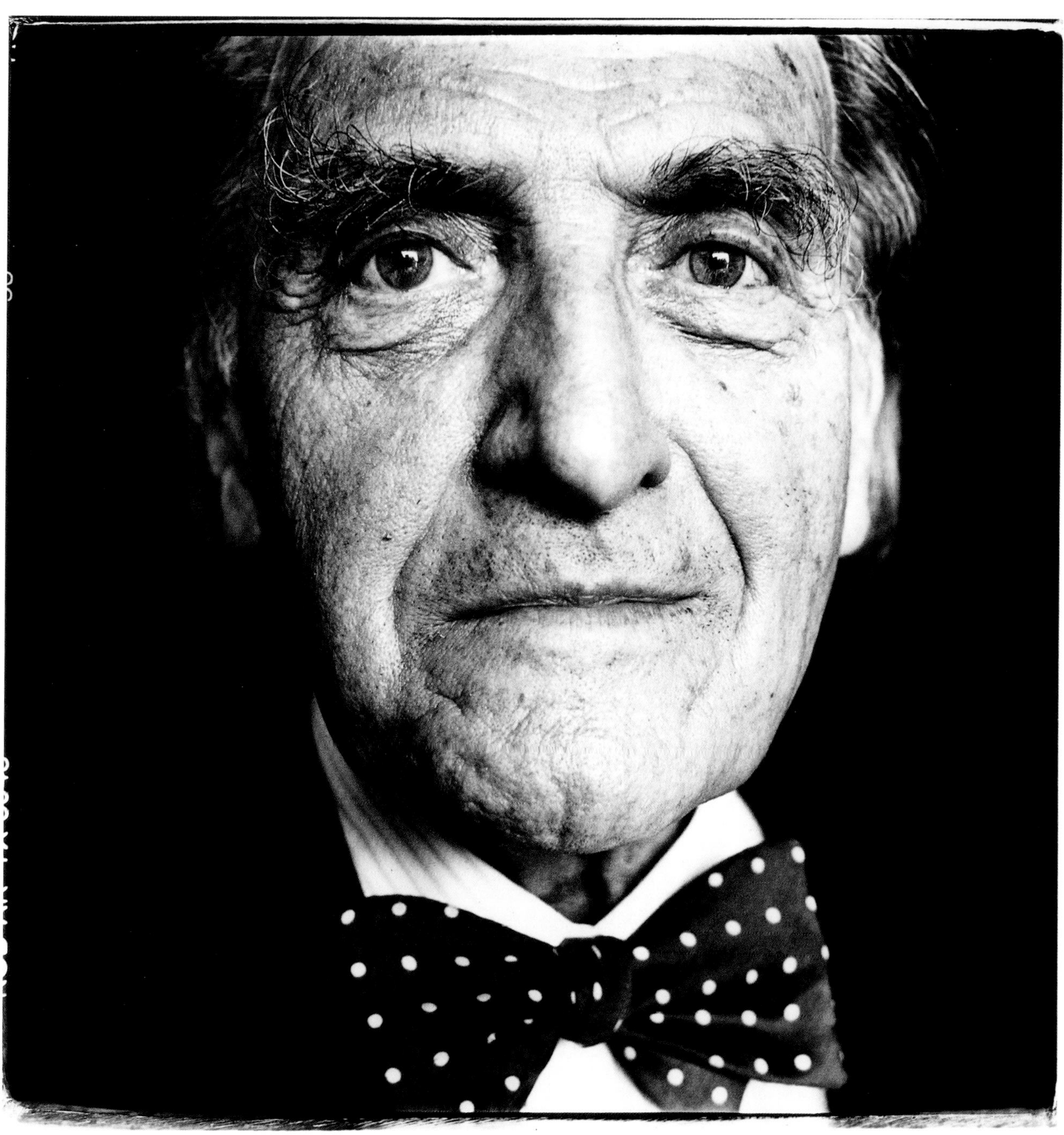

**Professeur Emmanuel Levinas**

*Paris, 7 December 1991*

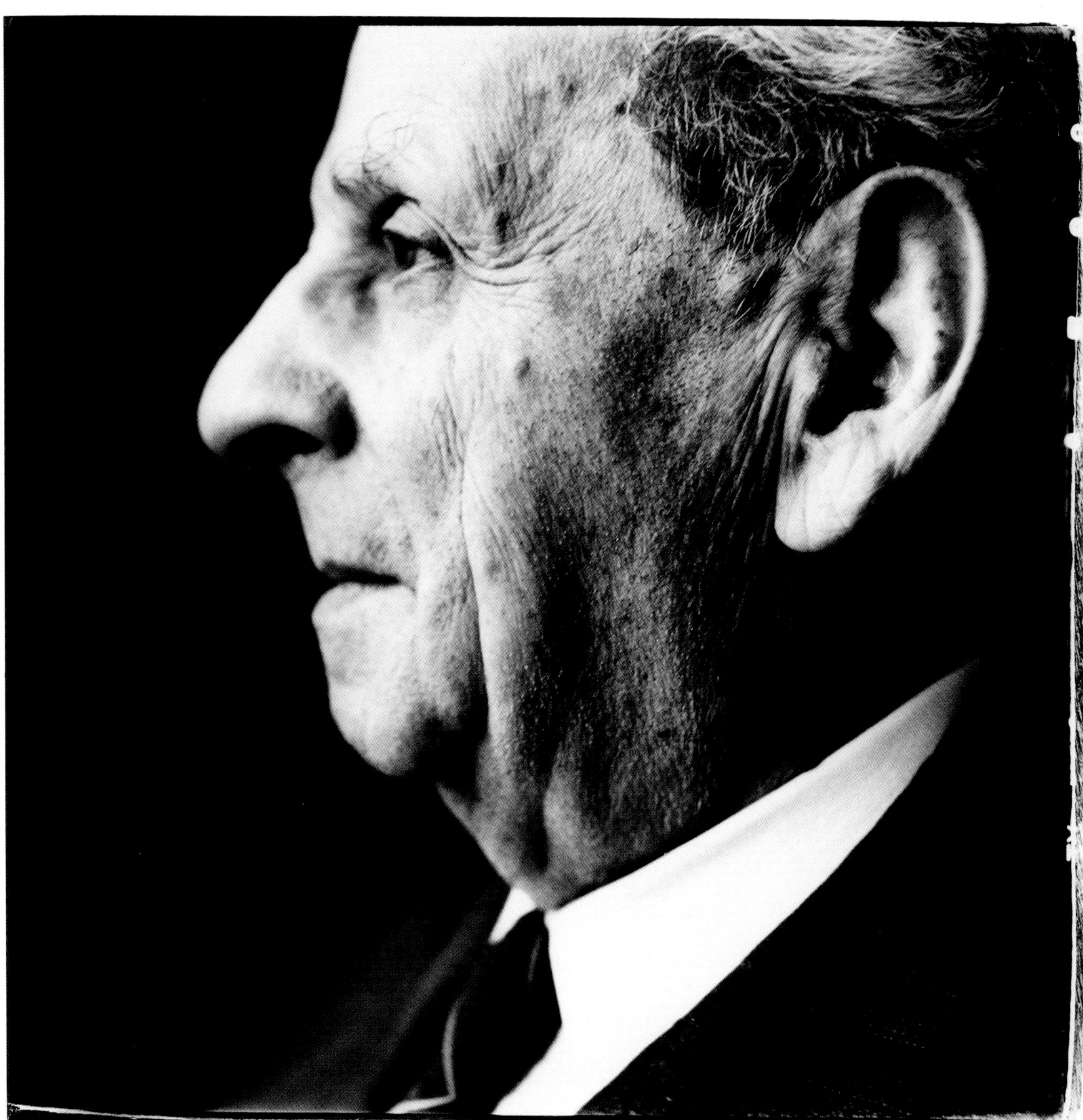

**Professor David Lewis**

*Princeton, 26 May 1990*

"I am an old-fashioned analytic metaphysician, in pursuit of hypotheses about what things are the elements of being, and about how all else may be reduced to patterns of these elements. I am notorious for claiming that these elements must include many that are merely possible, no part of this world that we ourselves live in, but none the worse for that. Apart from that, I am philosophically conservative: I think philosophy cannot credibly challenge either the positive convictions of common sense or the established theses of the natural sciences and mathematics."

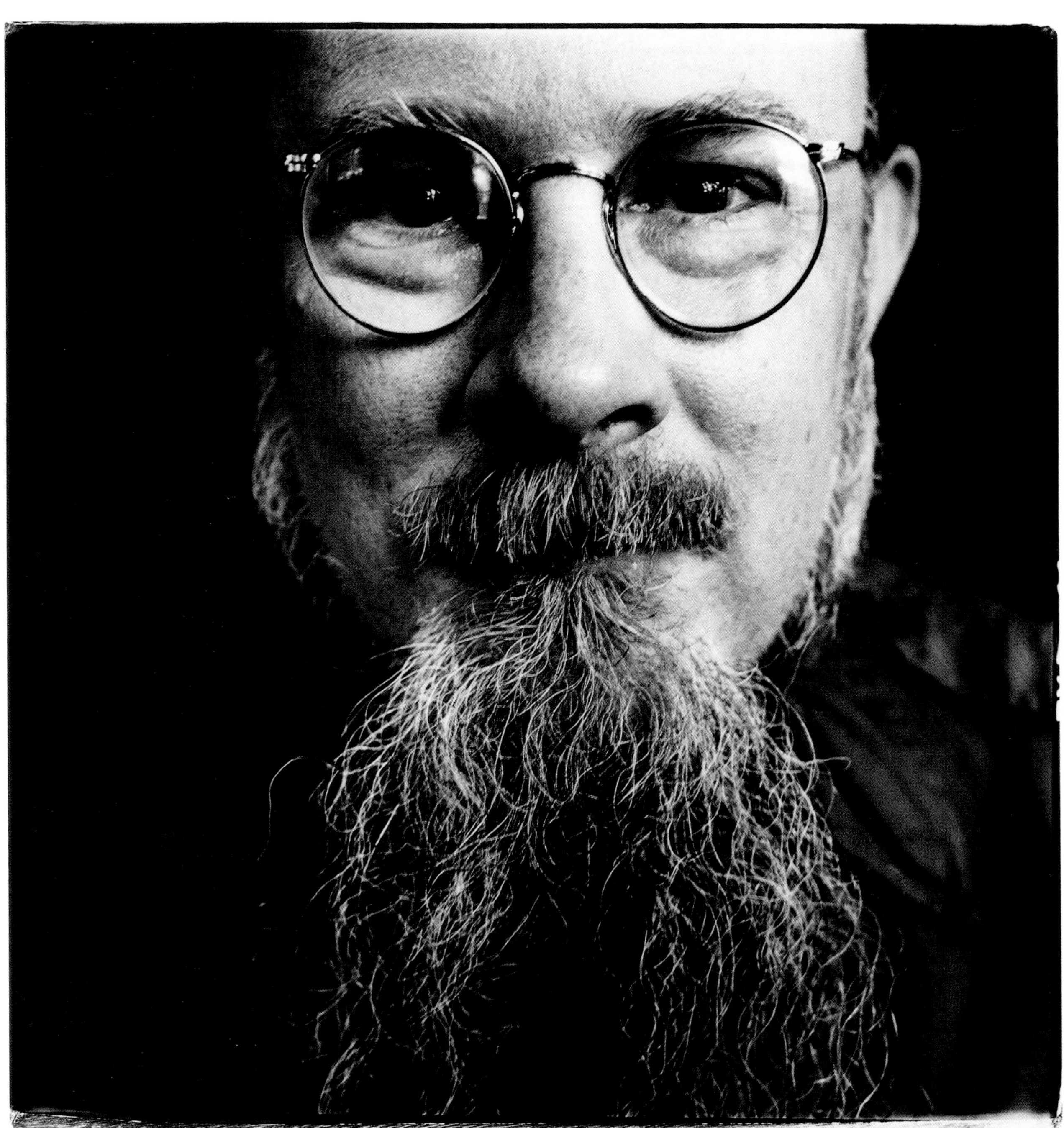

**Professor Cassimere Lewy**

*Cambridge, 1 August 1990*

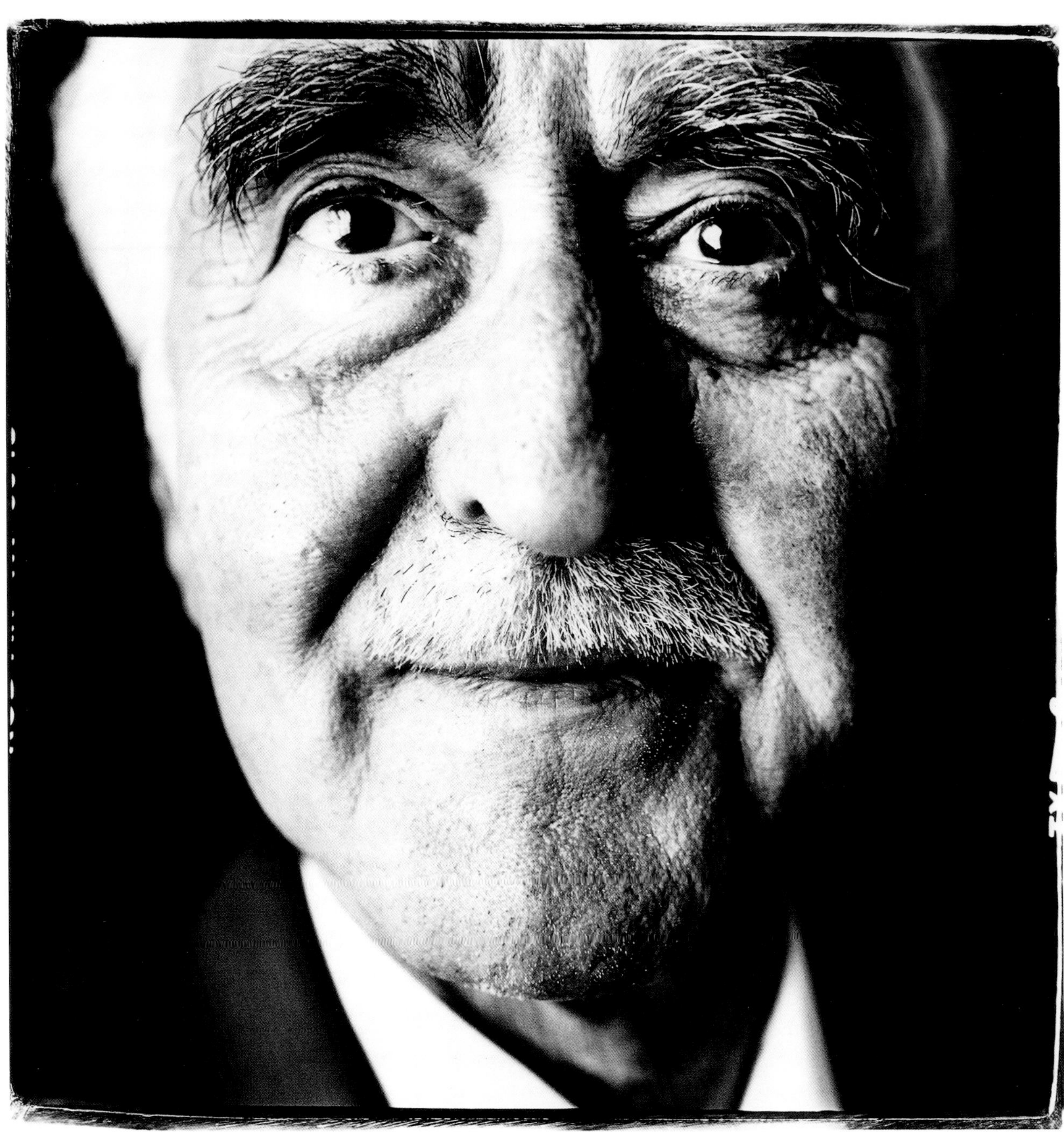

**Professor John McDowell**

*London, 14 June 1990*

"My main concerns in philosophy centre on the effects of a metaphysical outlook into which
we easily fall, at the point in the history of thought that we occupy. This outlook might be
called naturalism or scientism. I believe it tends towards a distortion of our thinking about the
place of mind in the world: the damaging effects show up not only in metaphysics itself, but
also (for instance) in reflection about language, and in the philosophy of value and action. The
task of philosophy, as I see it, is to undo such distortions."

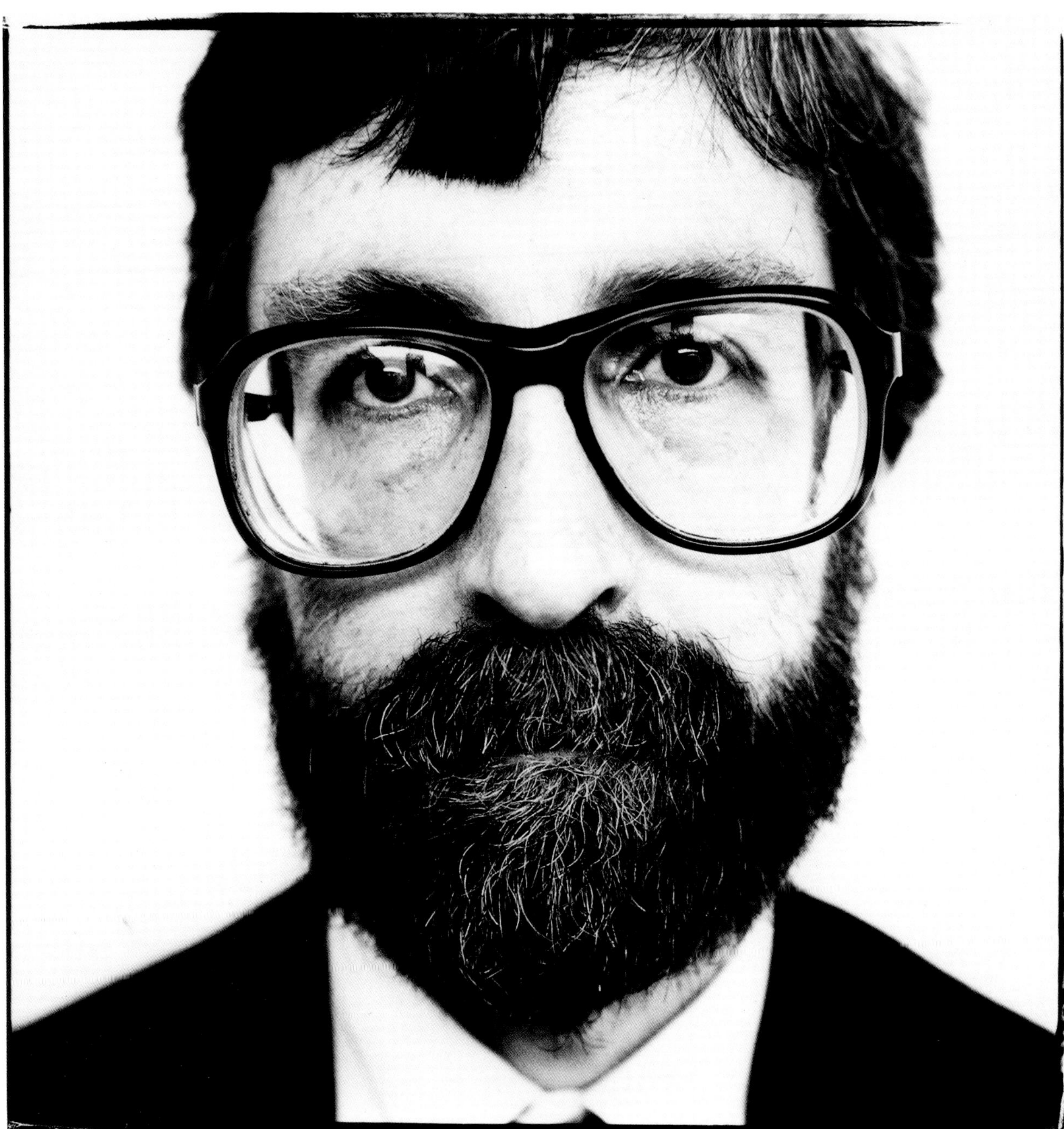

**Professor Alasdair MacIntyre**

*London, 24 March 1992*

"In philosophy there is always more to be learned from our predecessors, especially from Plato, Aristotle and Aquinas. But we often can only learn from them by reading their texts with our own new questions in mind. The problem is always that of knowing how exactly to formulate the questions."

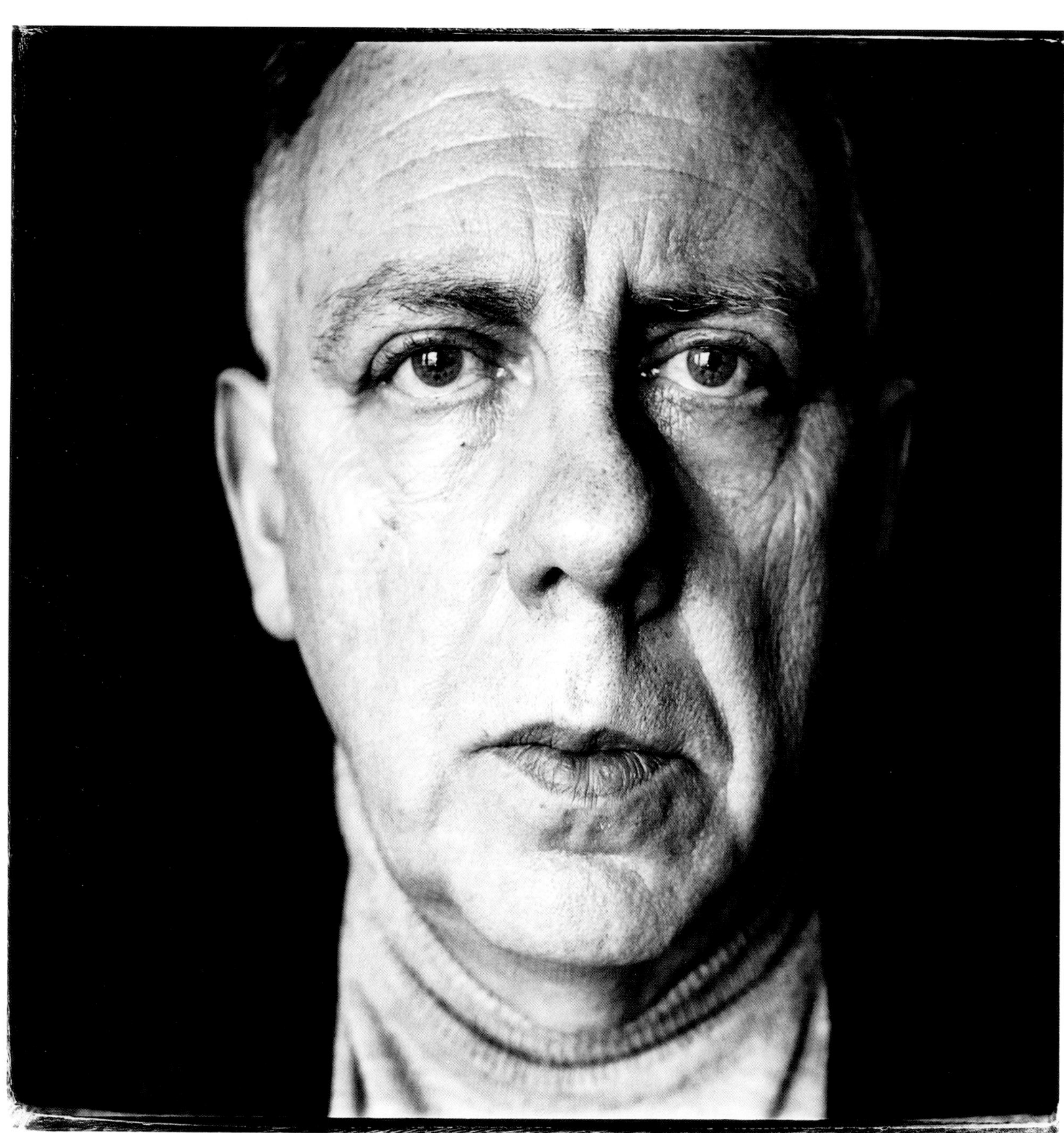

**Professor A Margalit**

*Oxford, 23 August 1990*

"What is philosophy? …

The study for self-knowledge.

Philosophy for me **now** is a form of social criticism."

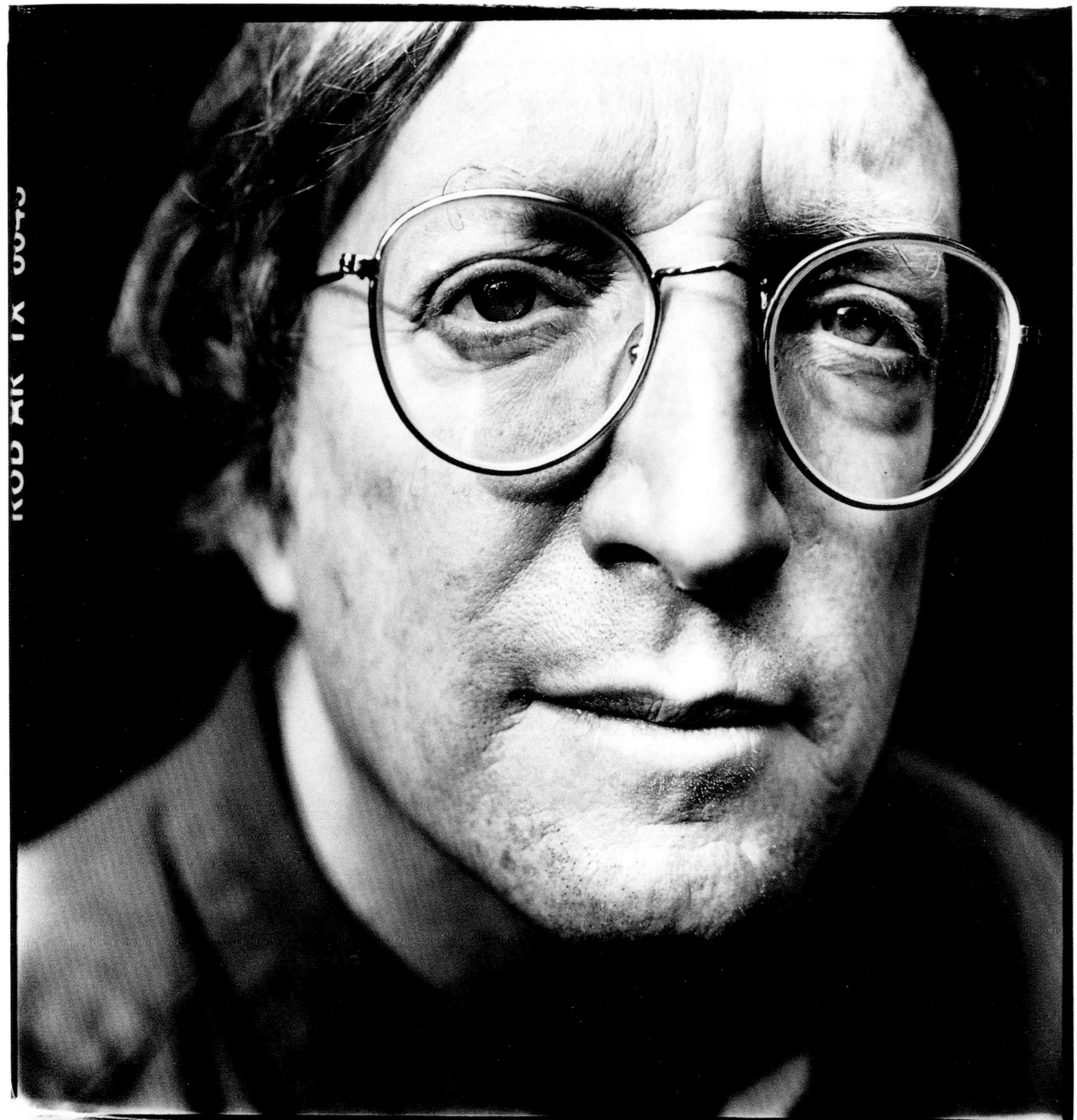

**Professor Hugh Mellor**

*Cambridge, 25 May 1990*

"I regard myself as a modern metaphysician, following a long Cambridge tradition (exemplified by Bertrand Russell and others) of basing my metaphysics on modern science. I have worked in particular on the nature of chance, time, causation and the mind, taking account of relevant developments in microphysics, cosmology, evolution, psychology and computer science. But while I use the analytic techniques of modern philosophy to expose and elaborate the metaphysical implications of modern science, I don't (unlike the logical positivists) think that metaphysics reduces to the analysis of science. Nor, unlike many modern analysts, do I think that it reduces to the analysis of language. On the contrary, I share the classical philosophers' belief that metaphysics is a serious discipline in its own right; and I have tried to show in my work how it has as much to teach the natural, social and linguistic sciences of our own day as it has to learn from them."

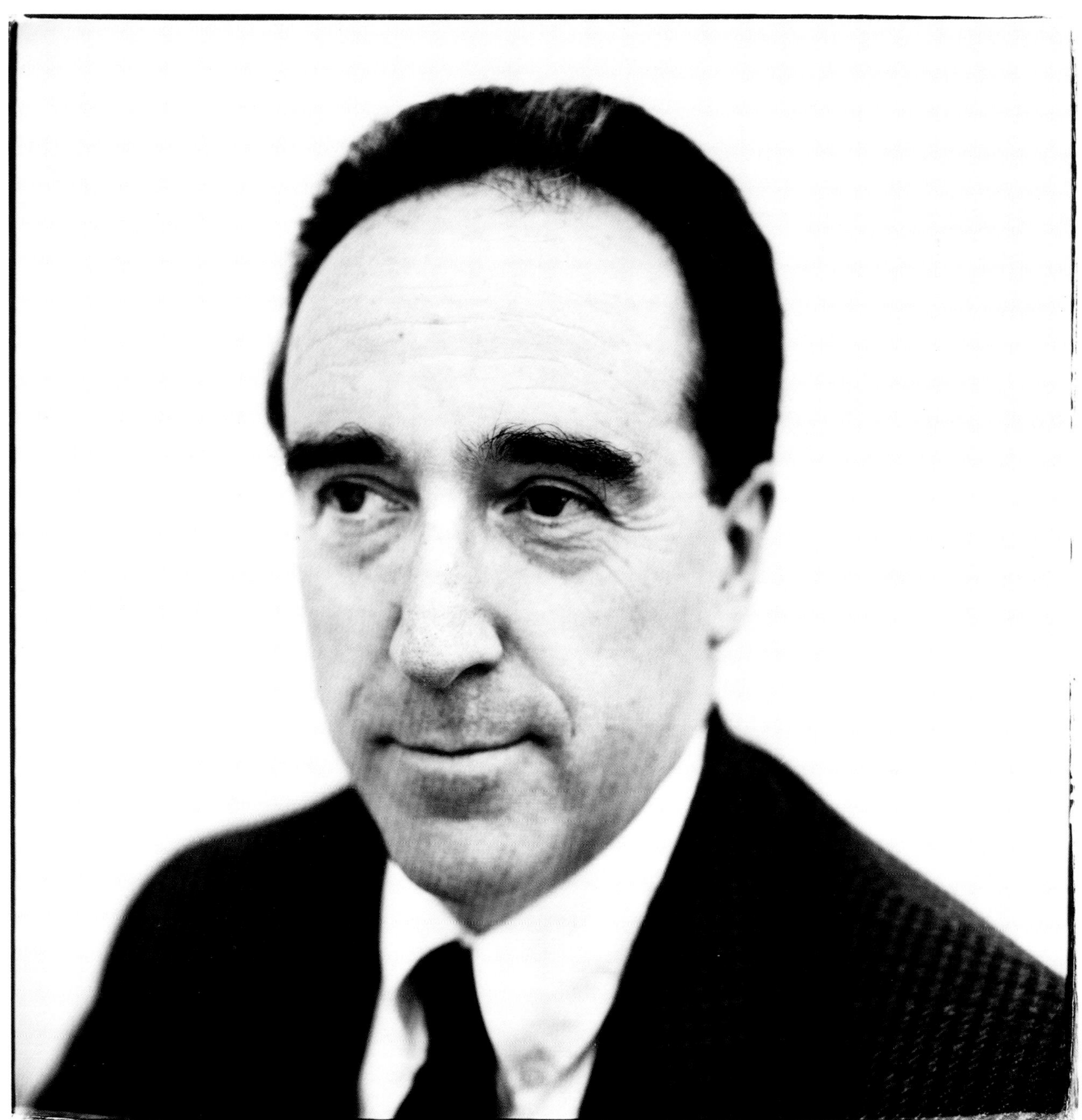

**Dame Iris Murdoch**

*Oxford, 13 November 1990*

"Our philosophical tradition, which goes back to Plato, is menaced in this technological post-Nietzchean age by a determinism which undermines our ethics and our concept of truth. Philosophy must not be allowed to fragment away into sociology, anthropology, psychology, logic and various forms of science. The planet needs philosophy. Human beings are moral beings: we must preserve a philosophical discourse which takes **this** as its fundamental subject matter. The great metaphysicians were great moralists. The centre must hold."

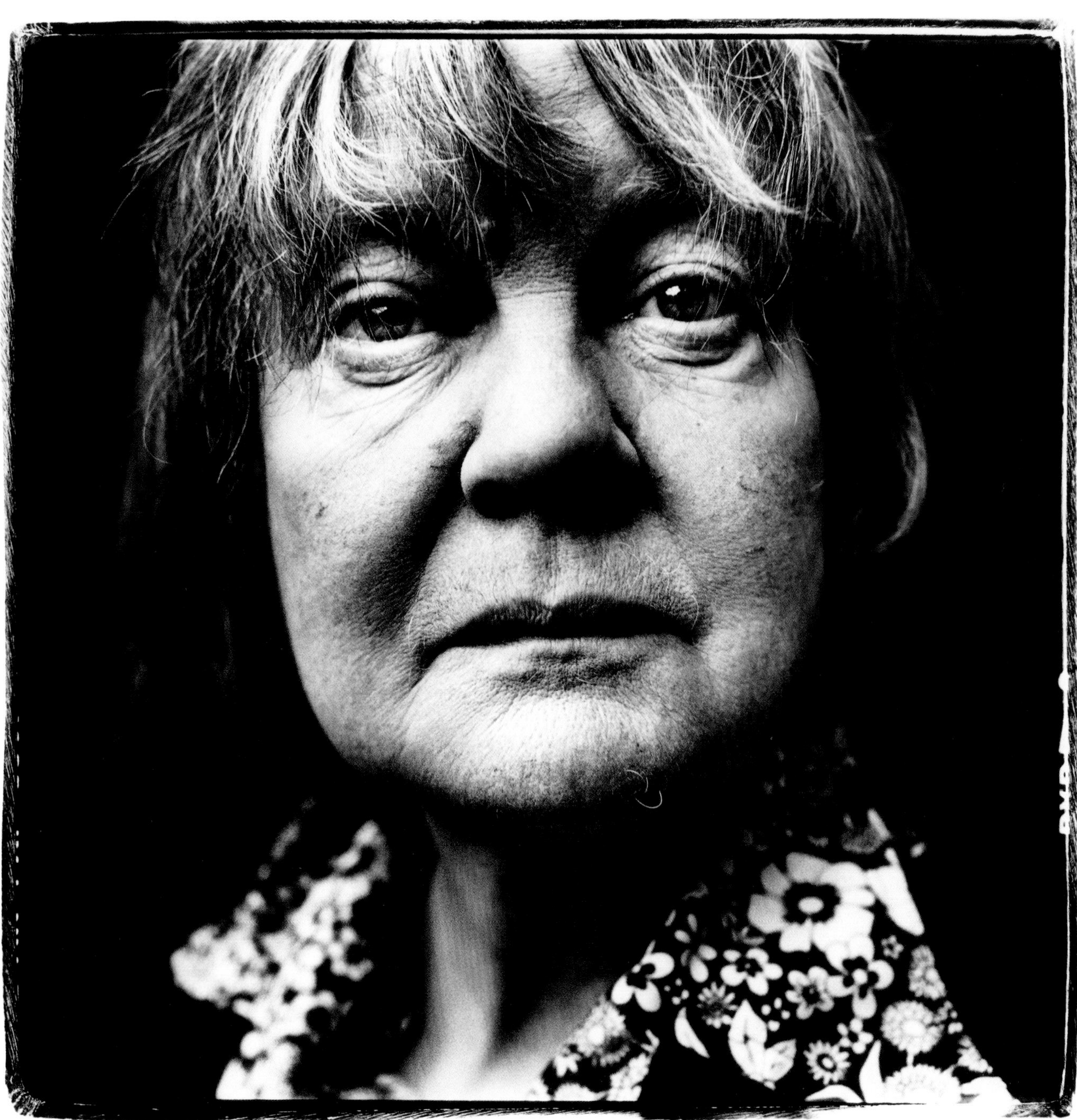

**Professor Thomas Nagel**

*London, 6 July, 1992*

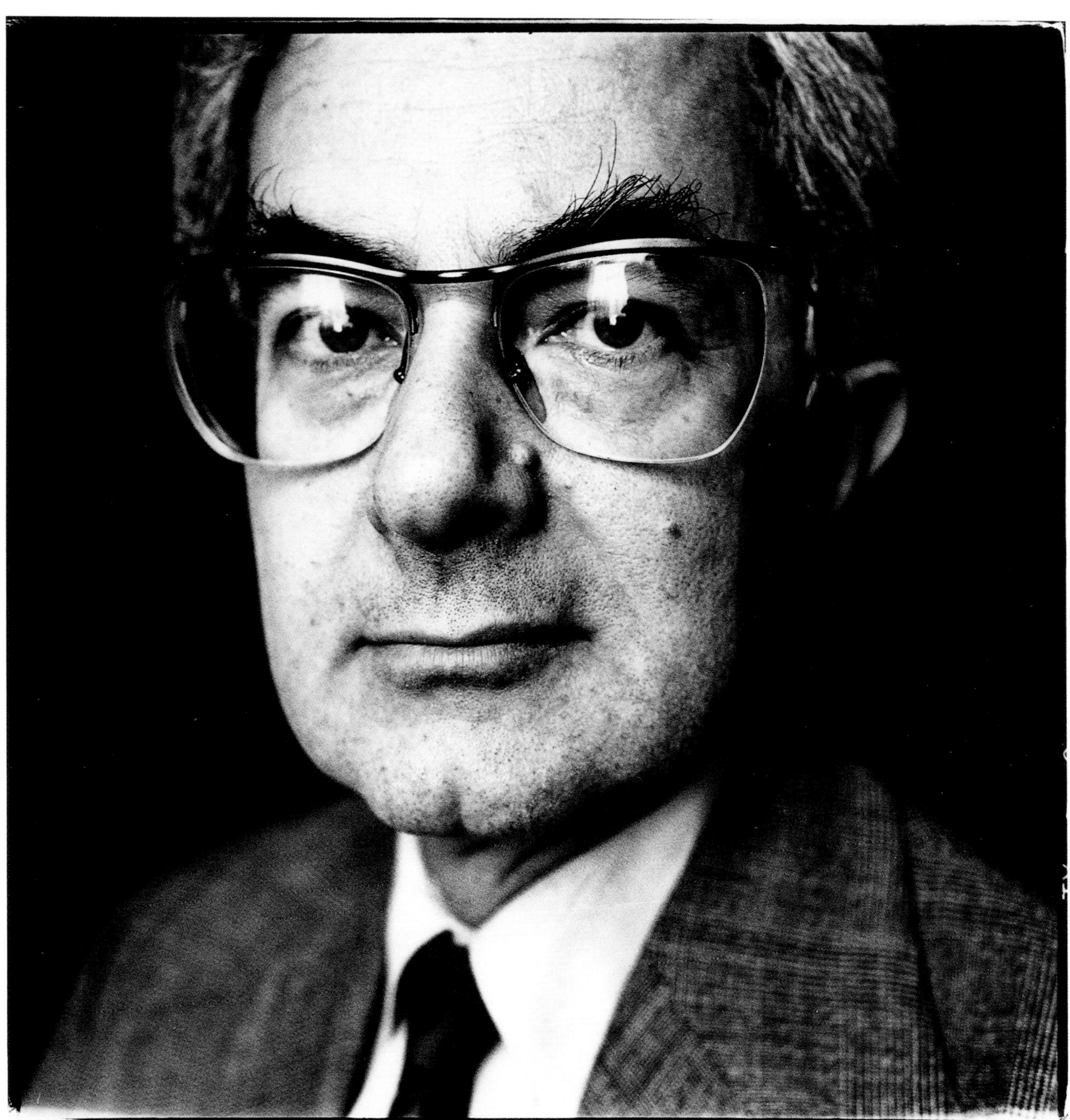

**Martha Nussbaum**

*London, 17 August 1992*

"Philosophy is an activity that uses reasoning and rigorous argument to promote human flourishing." *Epicurus*

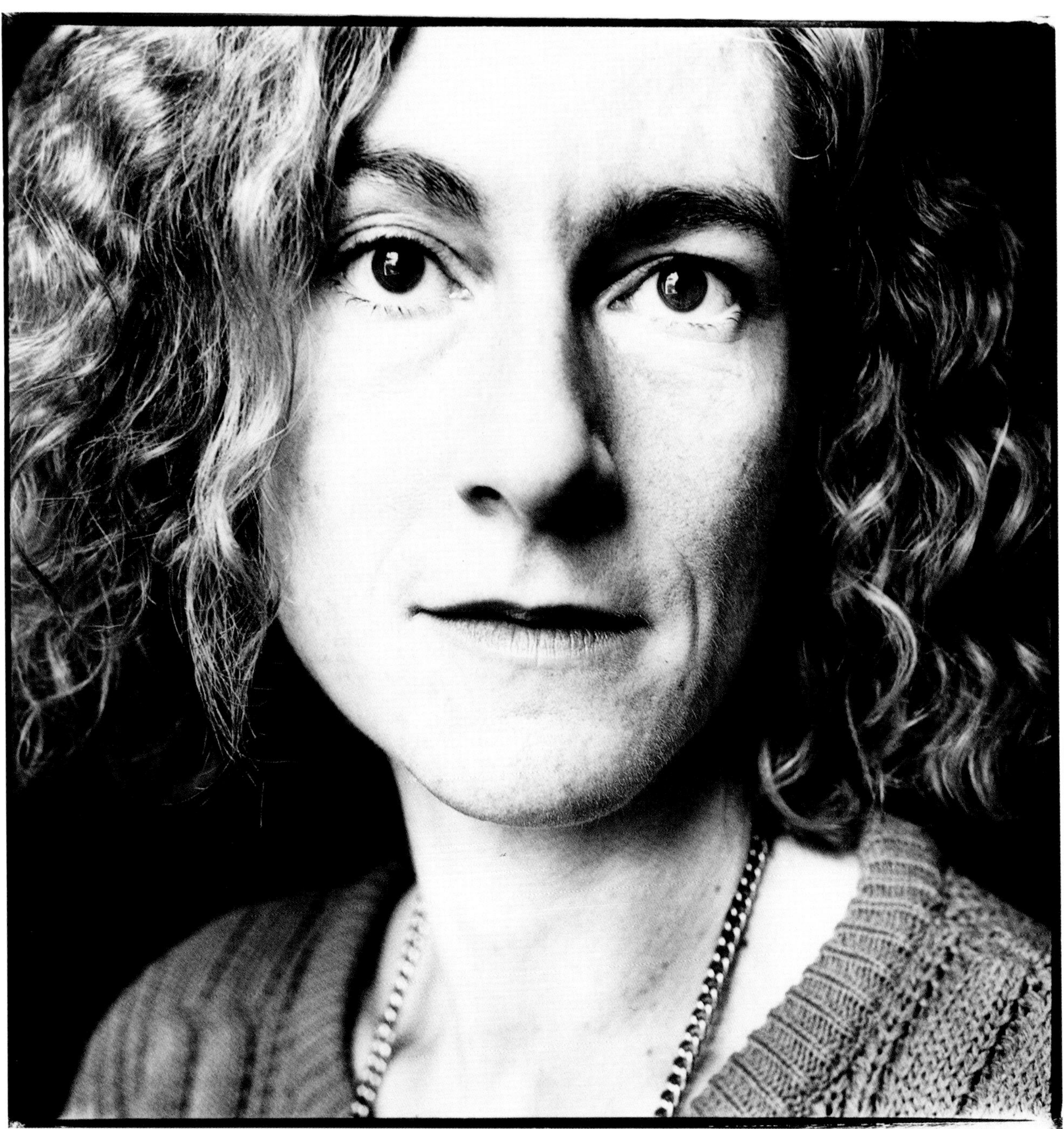

**Dr Onora O'Neill**

*London, 30 July 1992*

"'Consistency is the highest duty of a philosopher, yet the most rarely found': thus Immanuel Kant in his *Critique of Practical Reason*. Obstinacy rather than consistency may be the real hobgoblin of little minds; consistency rather than the complete truth as much as larger minds can reach."

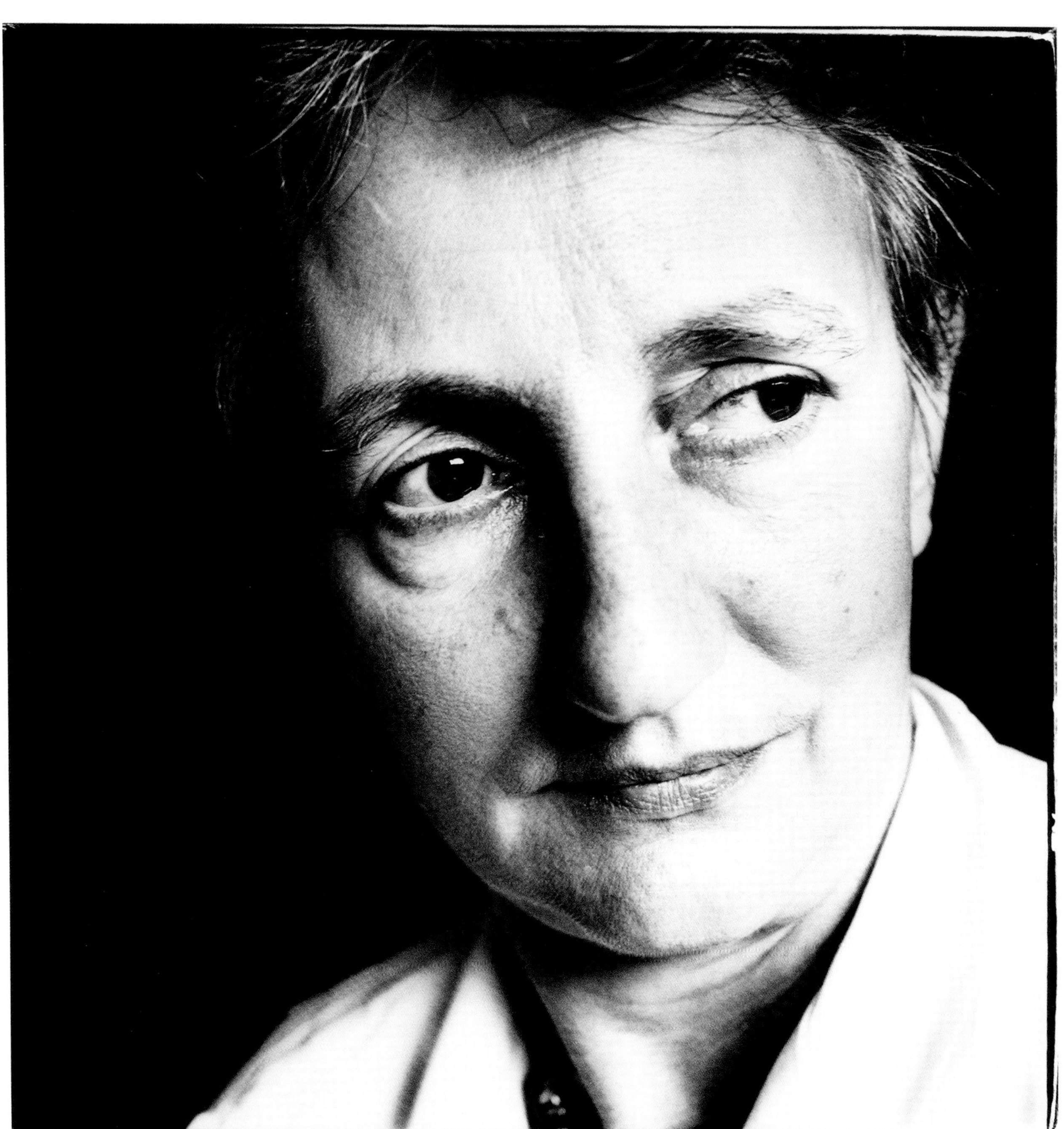

**Professor Derek Parfit**

*Oxford, 13 November 1990*

"What interests me most are the metaphysical questions whose answers can affect our
emotions, and have rational and moral significance. Why does the Universe exist? What makes
us the same person throughout our lives? Do we have free will? Is time's passage an illusion?"

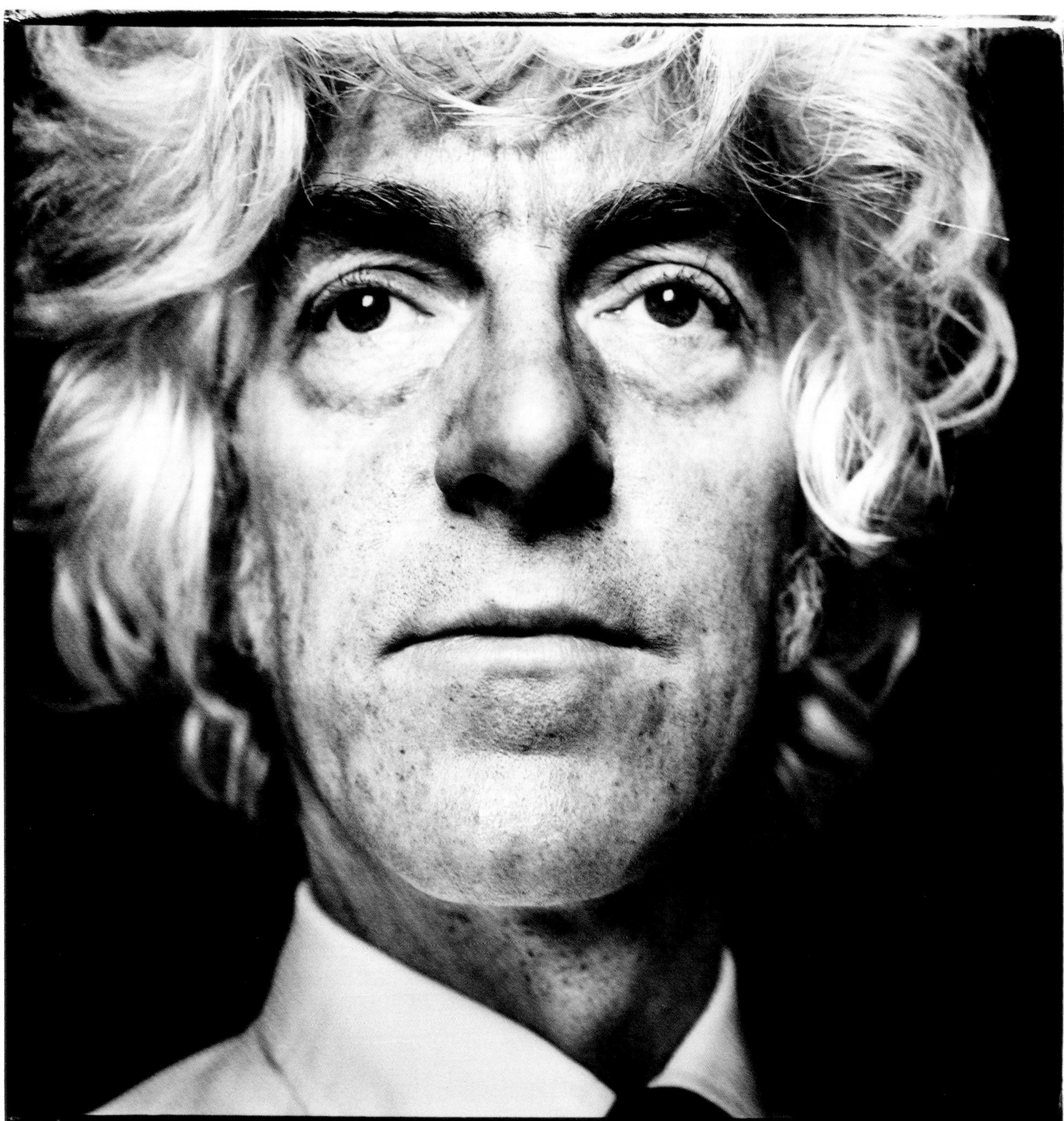

**Professor Günther Patzig**

*Göttingen, 3 November 1991*

"Philosophy is a methodical attempt to clarify fundamental concepts involved in human thought and action. The grave problems of the survival of our civilisation, even our species, cannot be solved without such rational inquiry. Against fashionable relativism and historicism, I side with Plato, Aristotle, Hume, Kant and Frege."

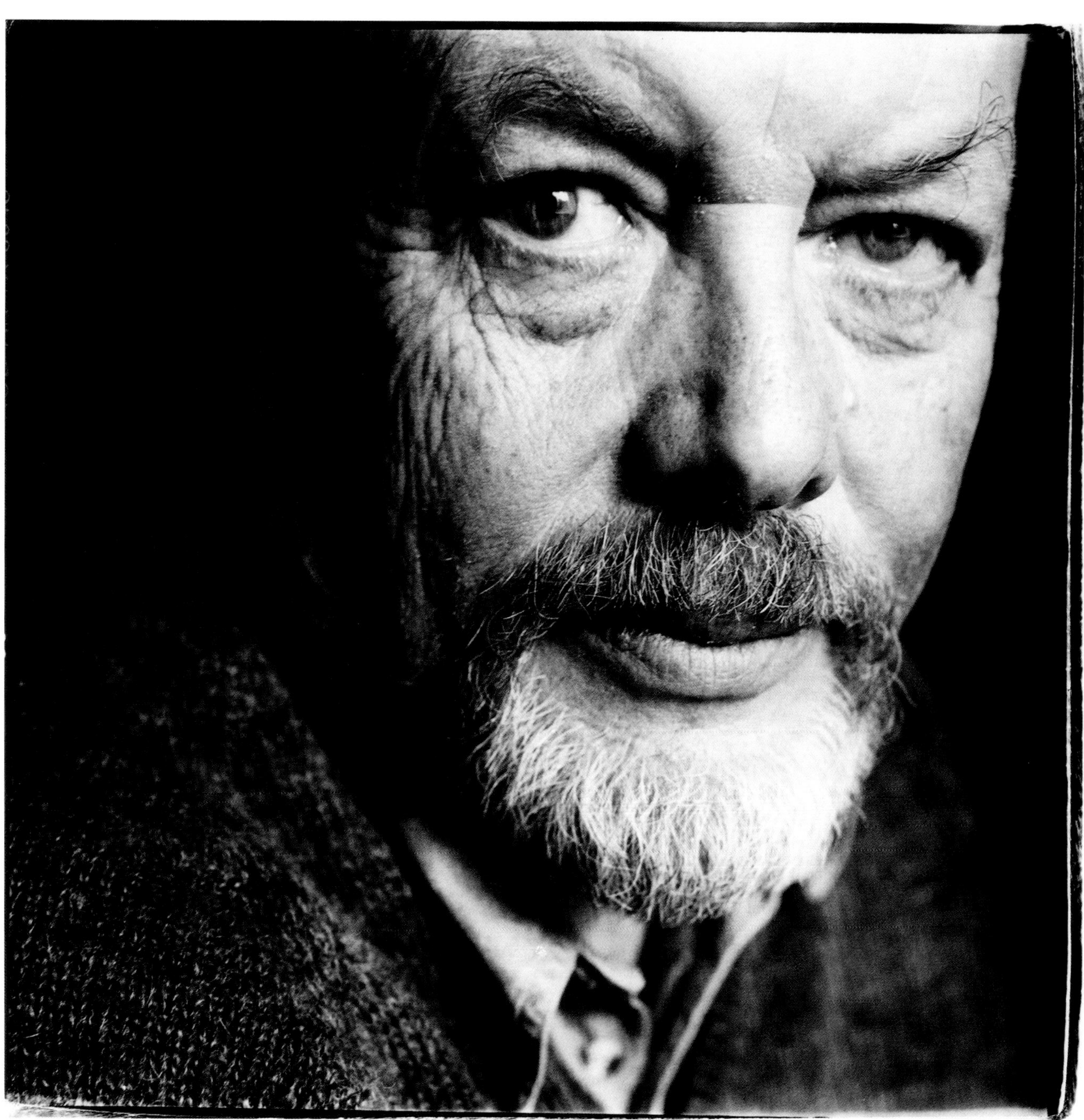

**Professor Christopher Peacocke**

*London, 10 March 1992*

"Christopher Peacocke has worked in the philosophy of mind, the philosophy of language and the philosophy of logic. He is currently working on a general theory of concepts, which is intended to address such questions as these: What is it for a thinker to possess a particular concept? How does an answer to this question allow our thoughts to be, on occasion, true though unverifiable? How is possession of concepts related to perception on the one hand and language mastery on the other? He believes that a framework which answers these questions properly has consequences for the theory of knowledge and for the proper way of conceiving of objectivity."

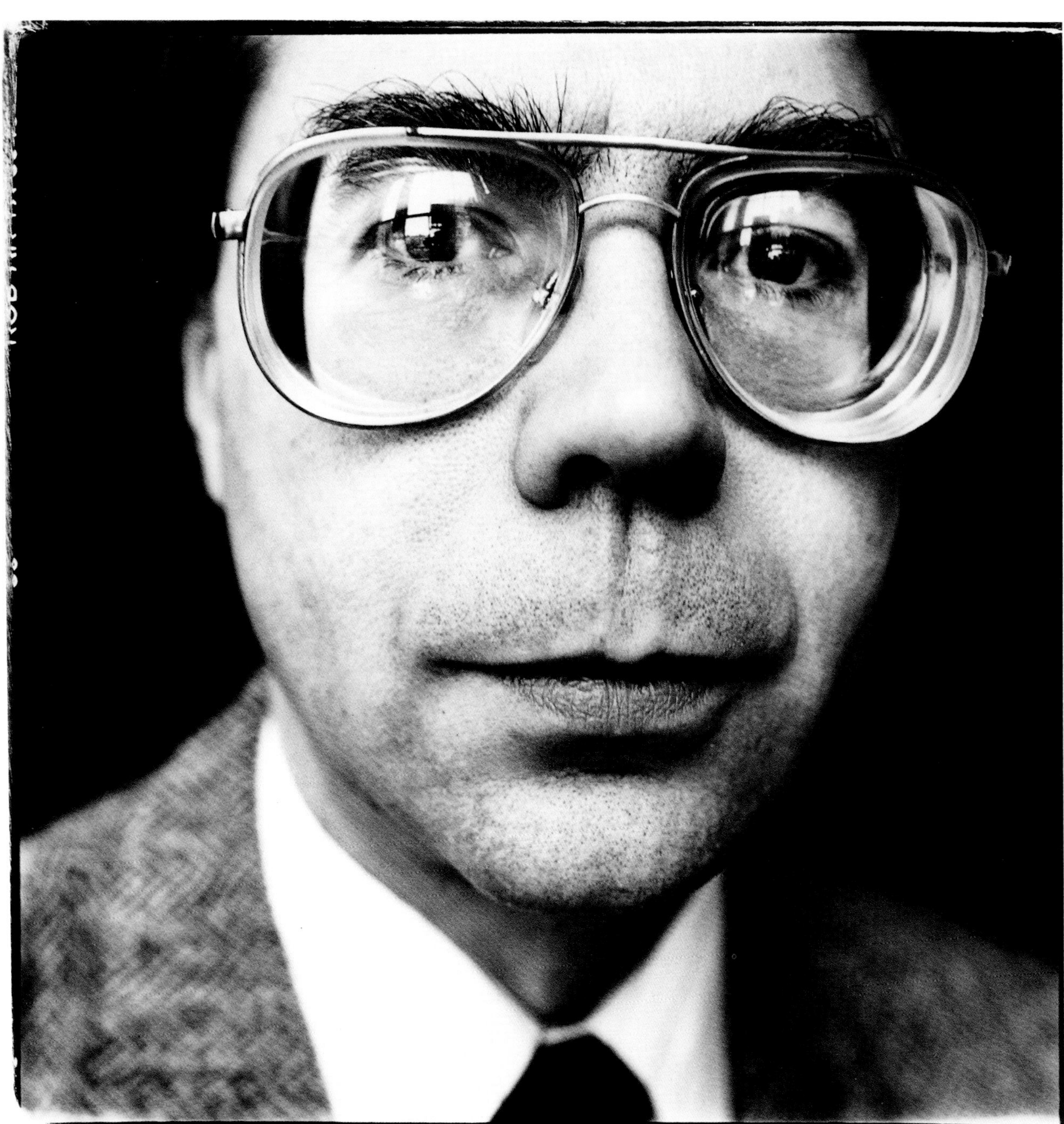

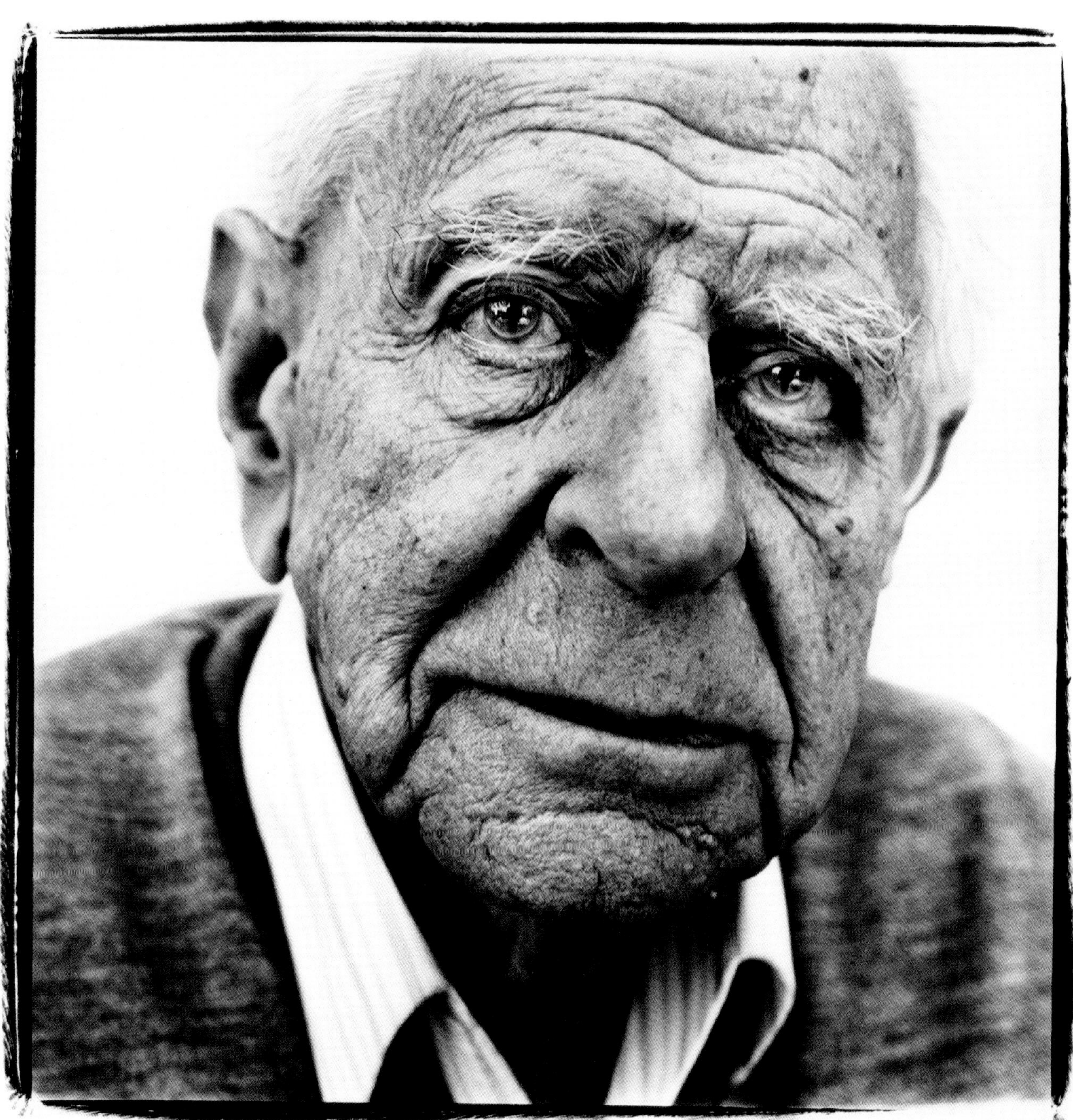

**Professor Graham Priest**

*Cambridge, 1 October 1990*

"Philosophy is that theoretical inquiry whose own nature falls within its scope."

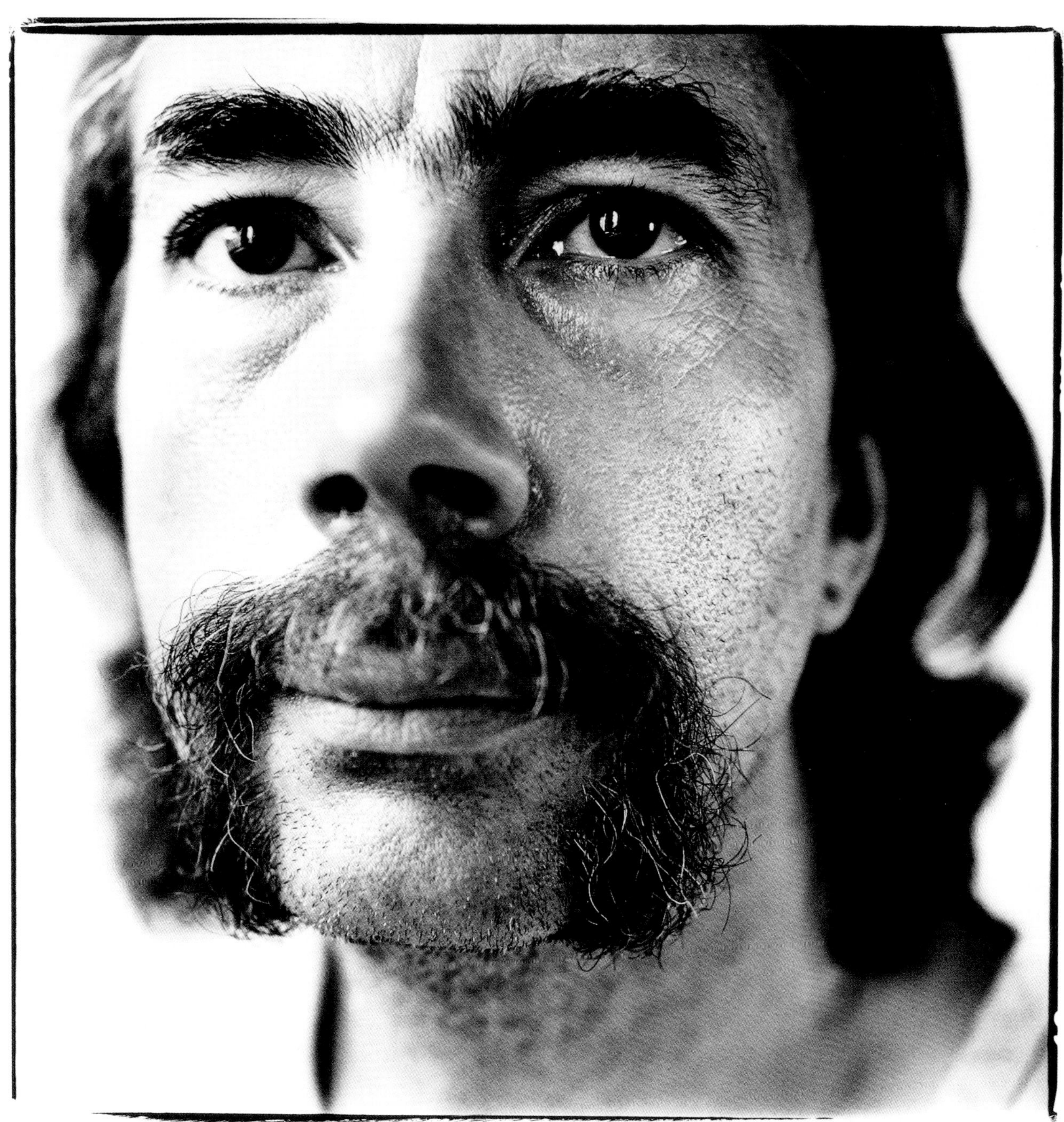

**Professor Hilary Putnam**

*London, 1 October 1990*

"The central long run philosophical problem facing people generally is how to maintain a belief
in progress without a belief in utopia."

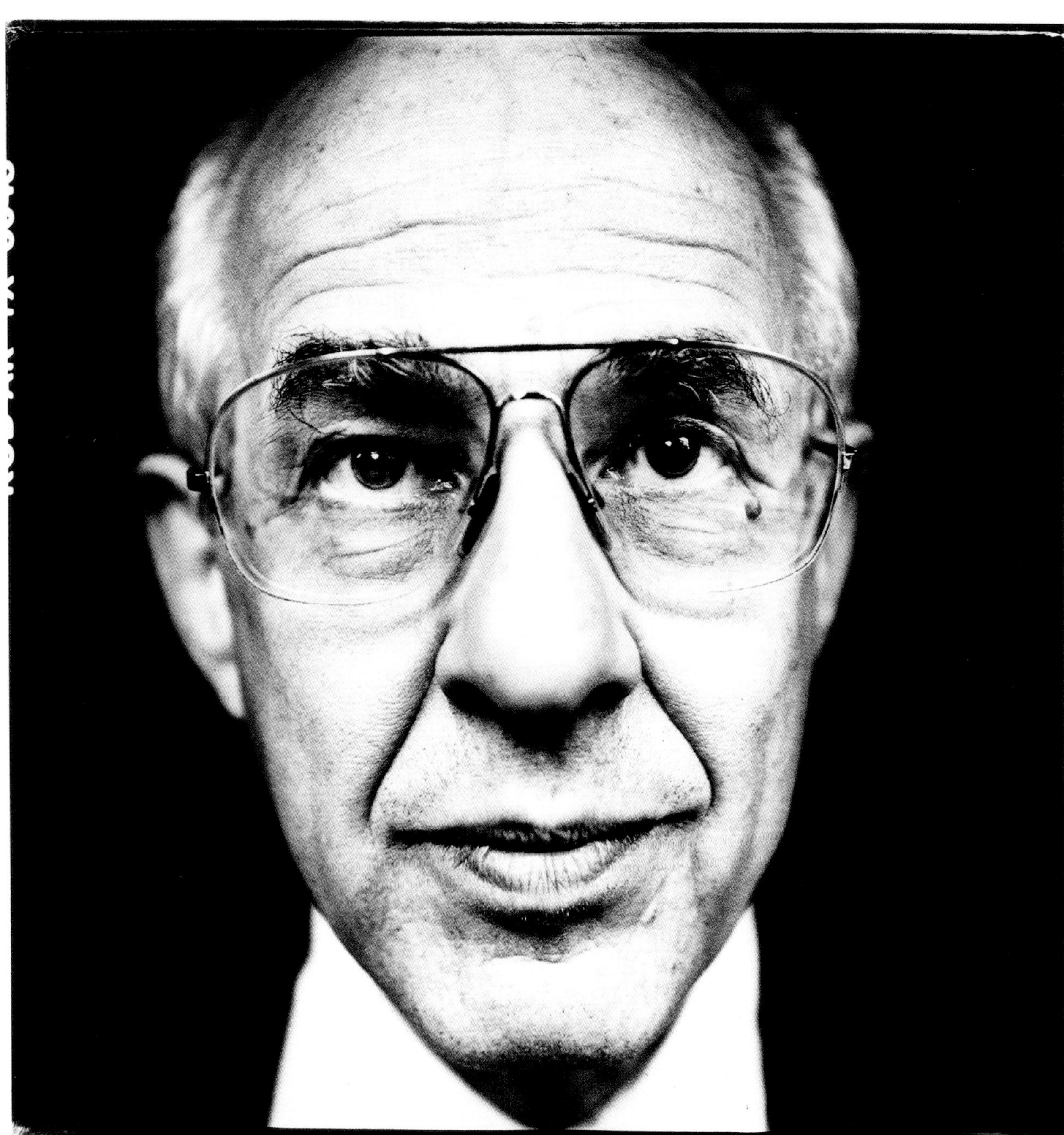

KODAK 5063 TX

**Professor W V Quine**

*Harvard, 29 May 1990*

"The world around us pelts our nerve endings with light rays and molecules, triggering sensations. Growing up in a garrulous society, we learn to associate patterns of these sensations with words and patterns of these words with further words until we reach the point somehow of talking about objects in the world around us.

We come to talk of animals, plants, planets, galaxies and also of the nerve endings themselves, the light rays and molecules. We talk of immaterial things too: numbers, classes and properties. I have sought a clearer view of the connections, logical and casual, between stimulation, language, and the natural world that language purports to describe. I have sought a clearer notion of why natural science turns out under experiment to be so largely true, and how much of it is imposed by man and how much by nature."

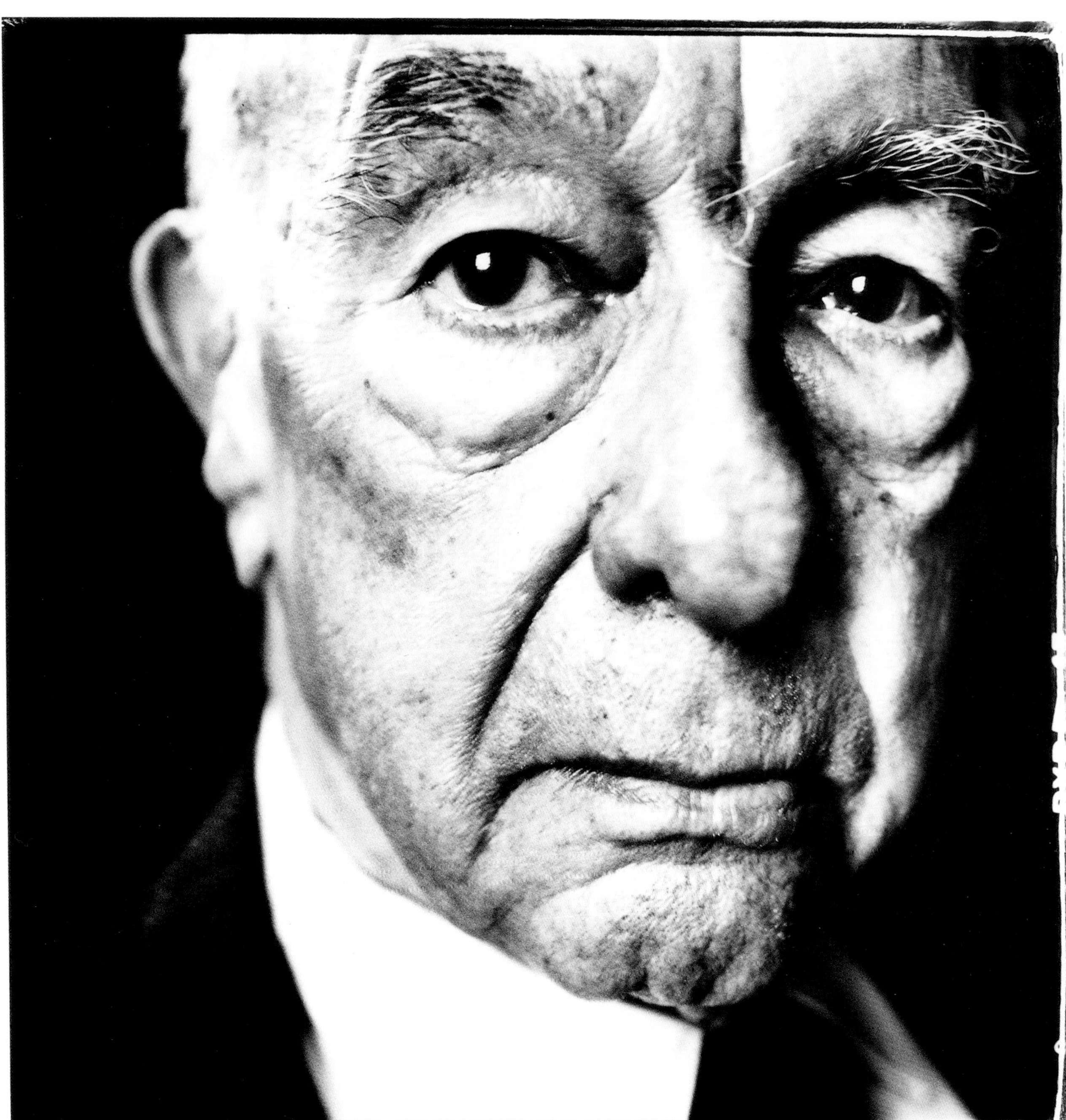

**Professor John Rawls**

*Harvard, 29 May 1990*

"From the beginning of my study of philosophy in my late teens I have been concerned with moral questions and the religious and philosophical basis on which they might be answered. Three years spent in the US army in World War II led me to be also concerned with political questions.

Around 1950 I started to write a book on justice, which I eventually completed."

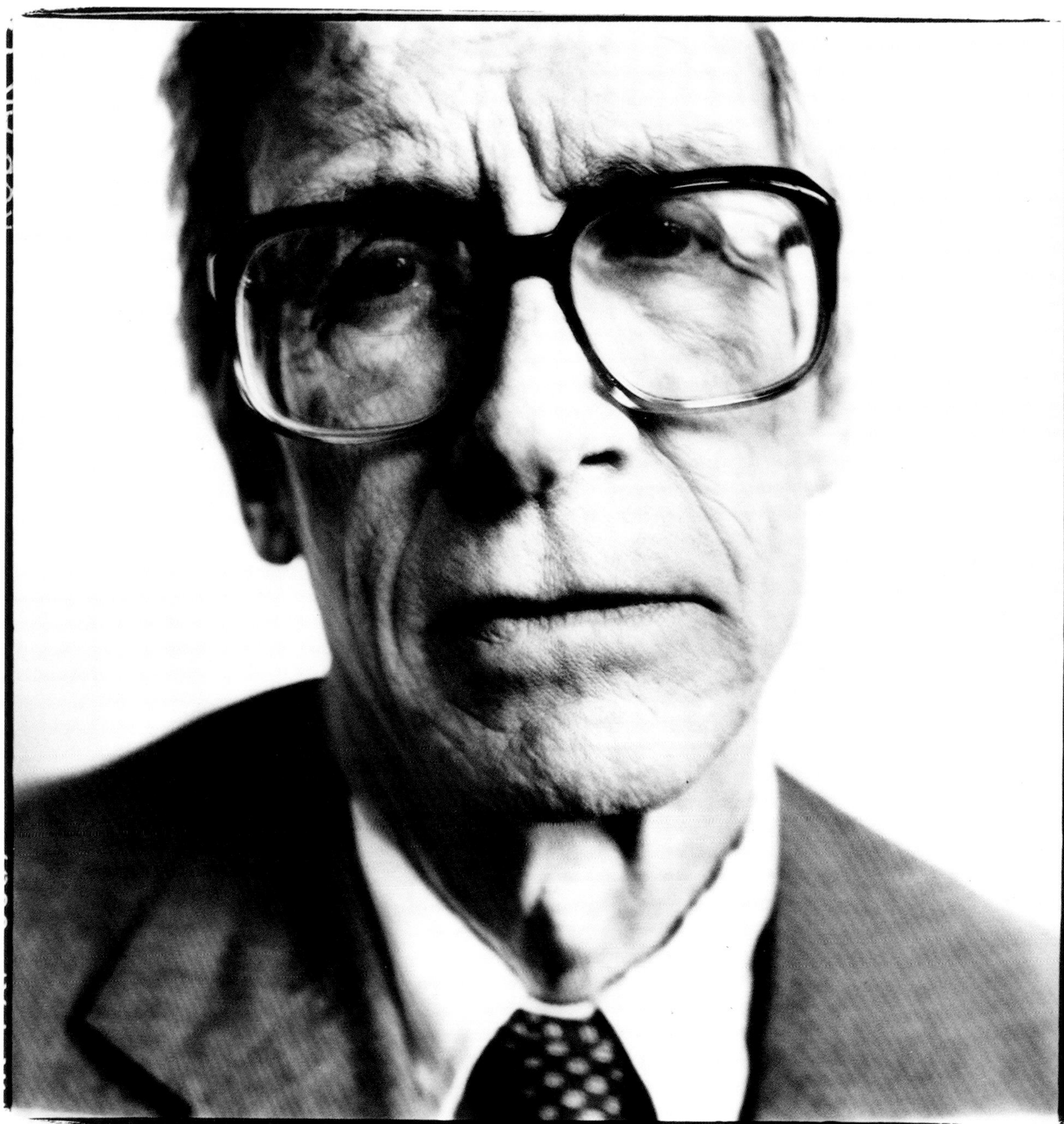

**Paul Ricoeur**

*Paris, 12 September 1990*

"To keep open the width of language."

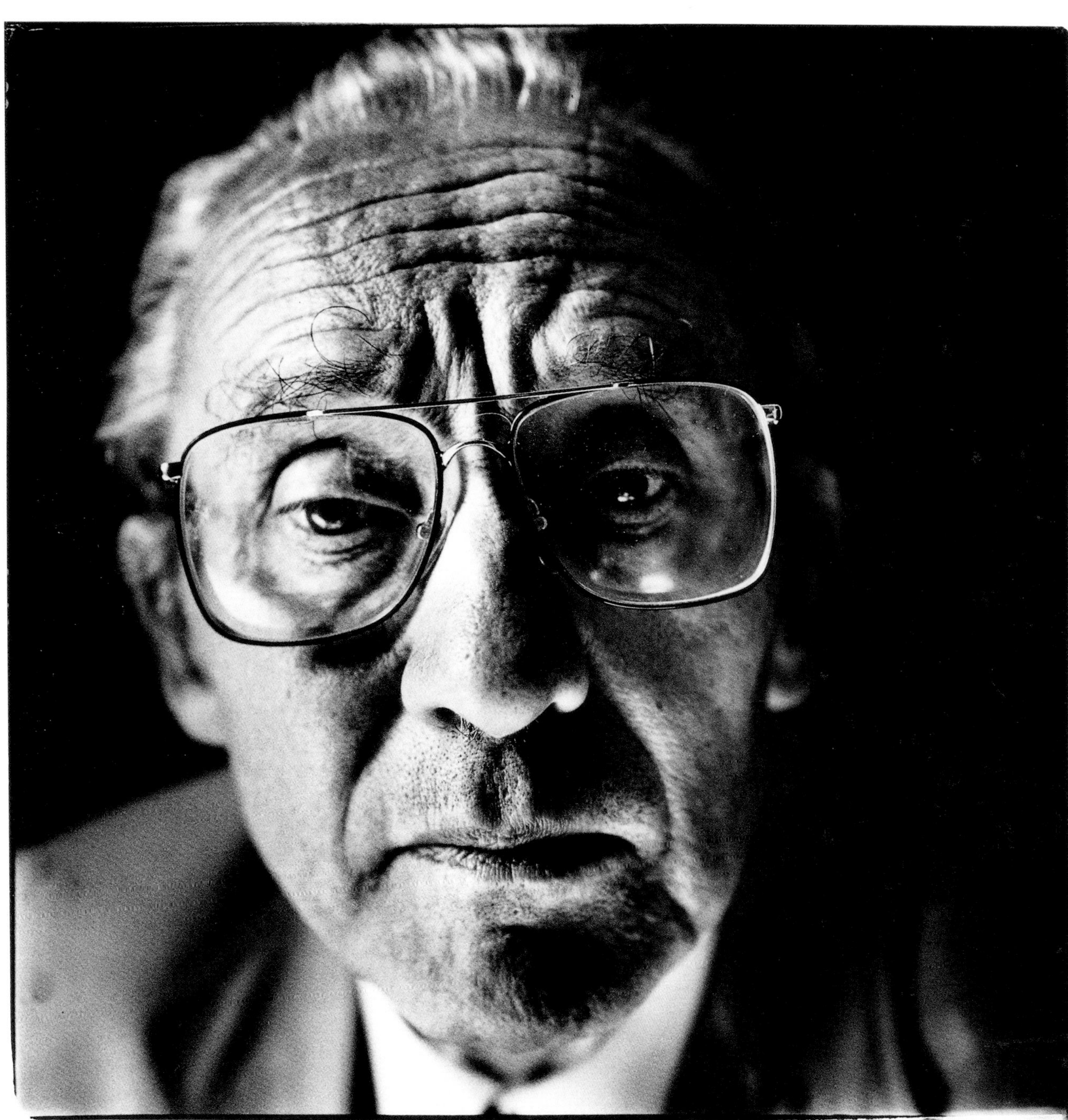

**Professor John Searle**

*London, 9 July 1992*

"If you can't say it clearly, you don't understand it yourself."

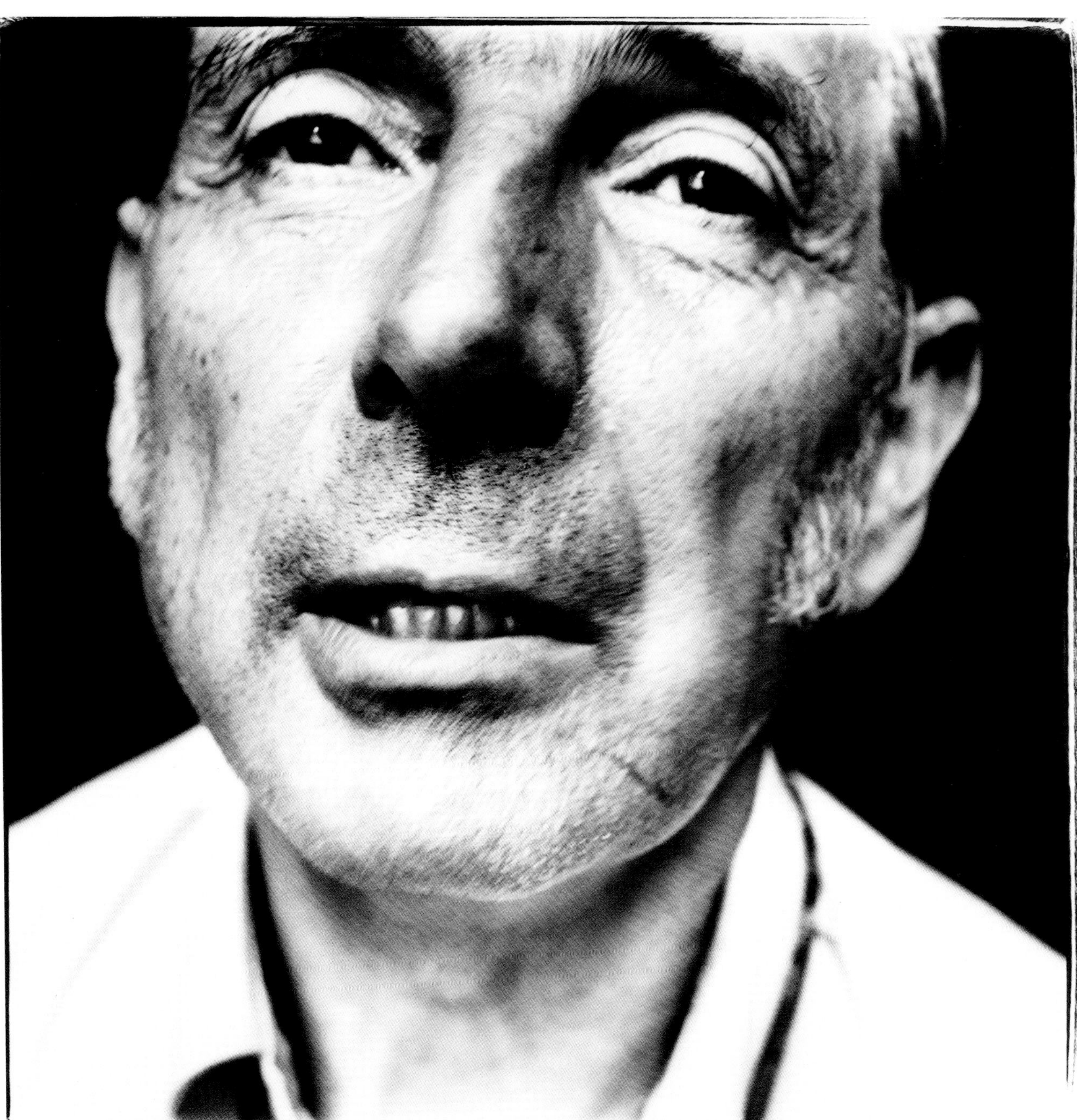

**Professor Amartya Sen**

*London, 8 August 1990*

"The Sanskrit word for philosophy – *darśana* – also means seeing clearly. Philosophy does have much to do with clarifying matters – not through specialized knowledge but through reasoning. It is possible, of course, to be wonderfully clear and dead wrong. But lucidity does not help the survival of baseless beliefs, silly deductions, groundless prejudice, or the justification of needless misery. Well, that's something for clear reasoning, even though it won't solve all our problems."

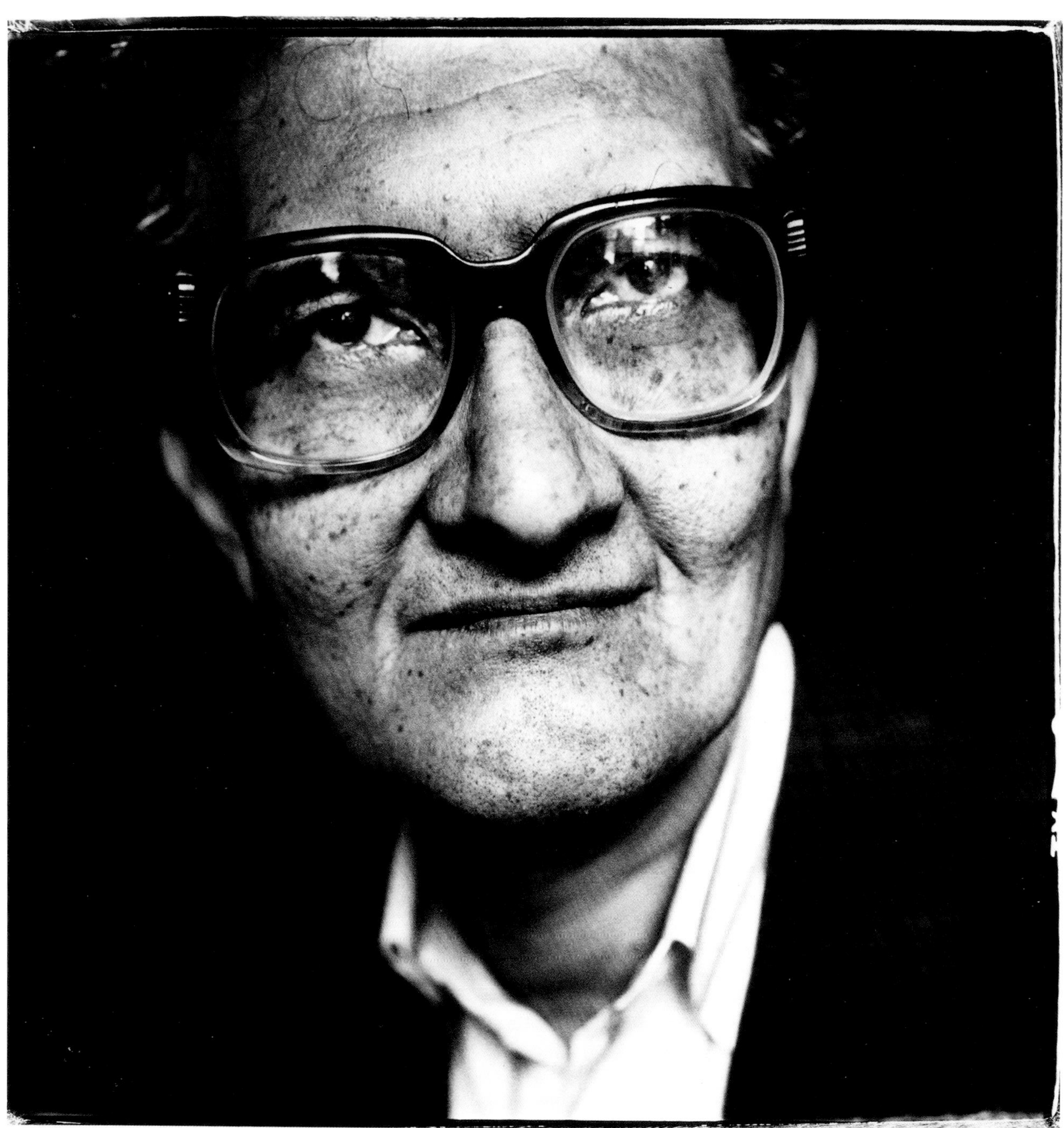

**Professor Timothy Smiley**

*Cambridge, 1 August 1990*

"I feel odd man out in a collection of philosophers, since my work is on logic and often mathematical. I suppose I do what I do from a mixture of curiosity and mischief — a reluctance to let sleeping dogs lie and a desire for clear-cut, unexpected results. Rehabilitating Aristotle's logic is satisfying on both counts."

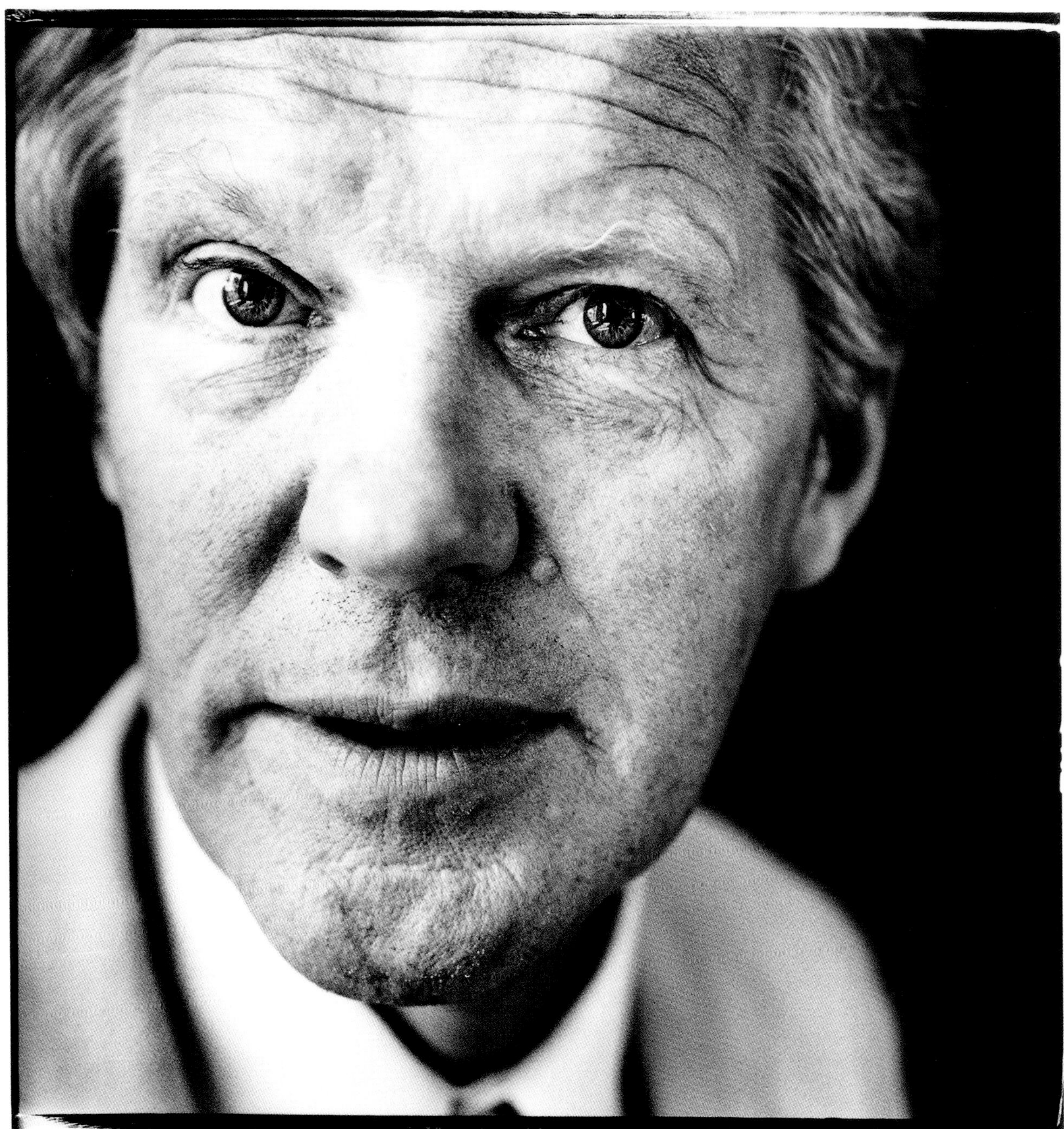

**Professor Sir Peter Strawson**

*Oxford, 21 May 1990*

"I take the philosophical aim to be that of elucidating the character and interconnections of the key concepts (eg those of identity, existence, truth, knowledge, meaning, cause, mind, body, space, time) which constitute the structural framework of all detailed human thinking. The aim, one could say, is that of conceptual self-understanding."

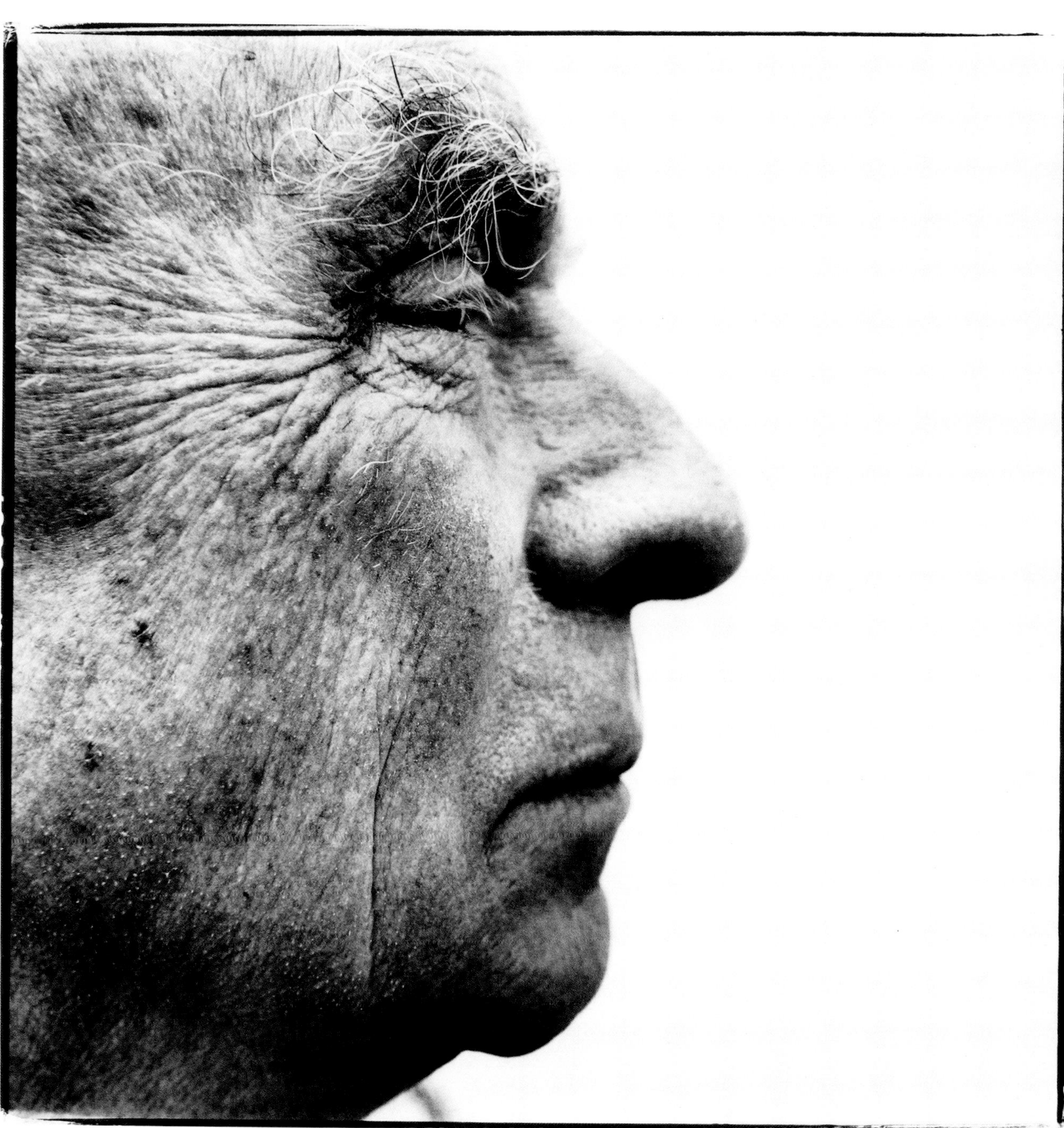

**Professor Richard Sorabji**

*London, 4 July 1990*

"For the historian of Philosophy, Philosophy matters. He or she draws from and gives to it.
Gives, because understanding a historical view correctly expands the philosophical imagination.
Even misunderstanding a historical view can be philosophically fruitful: Neoplatonism is a
distortion of both Plato and Aristotle. But eventually the historian must set the record straight,
and the cross-fertilisation between History and Philosophy will continue."

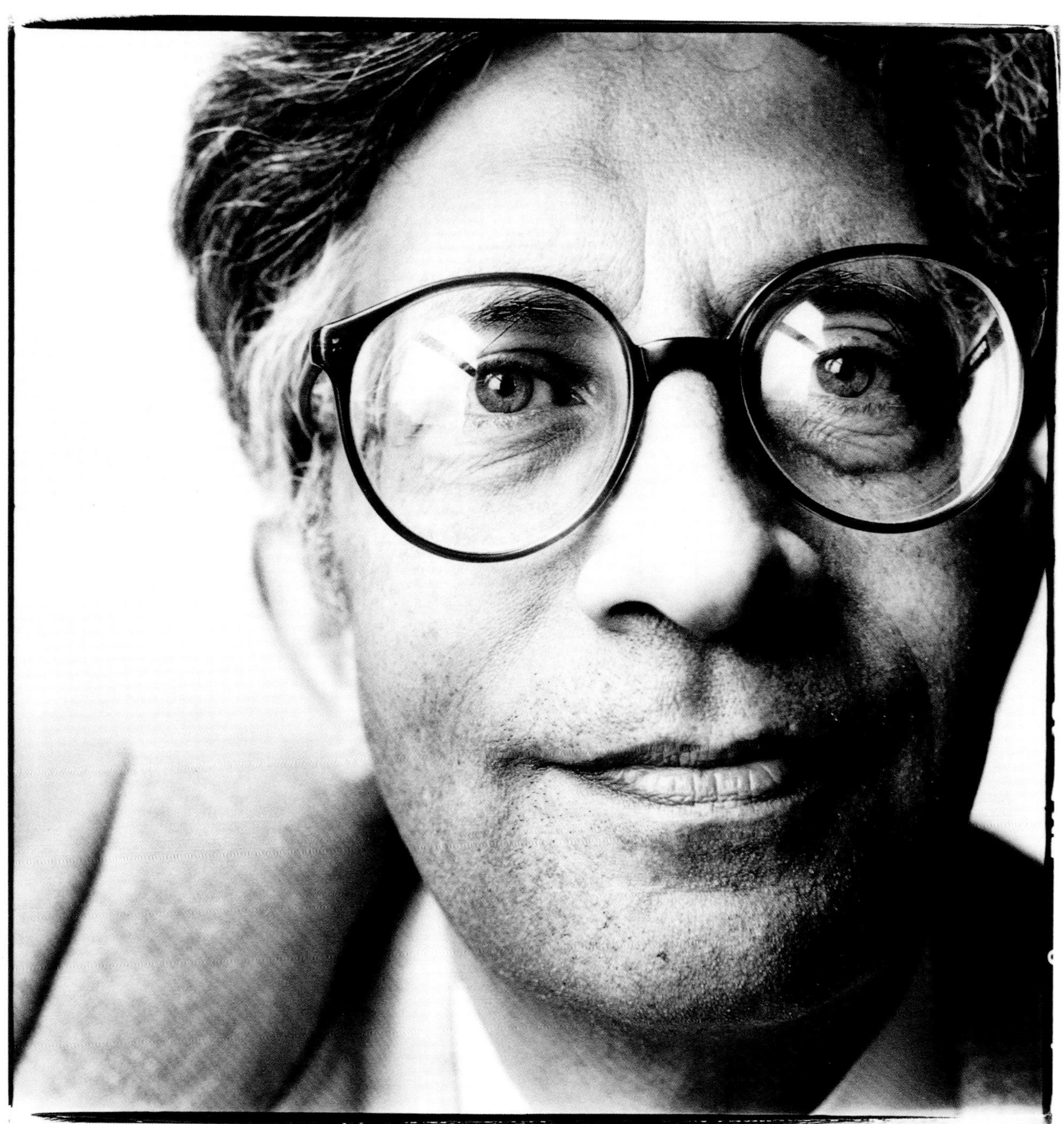

**Professor Charles Taylor**

*London, 8 June 1992*

"There are many different ways of doing philosophy, but what means most to me is articulating
what we half-know (and sometimes are tempted to ignore or deny) and then bringing that to
bear on the rest of what we know and want and do. It makes a difference."

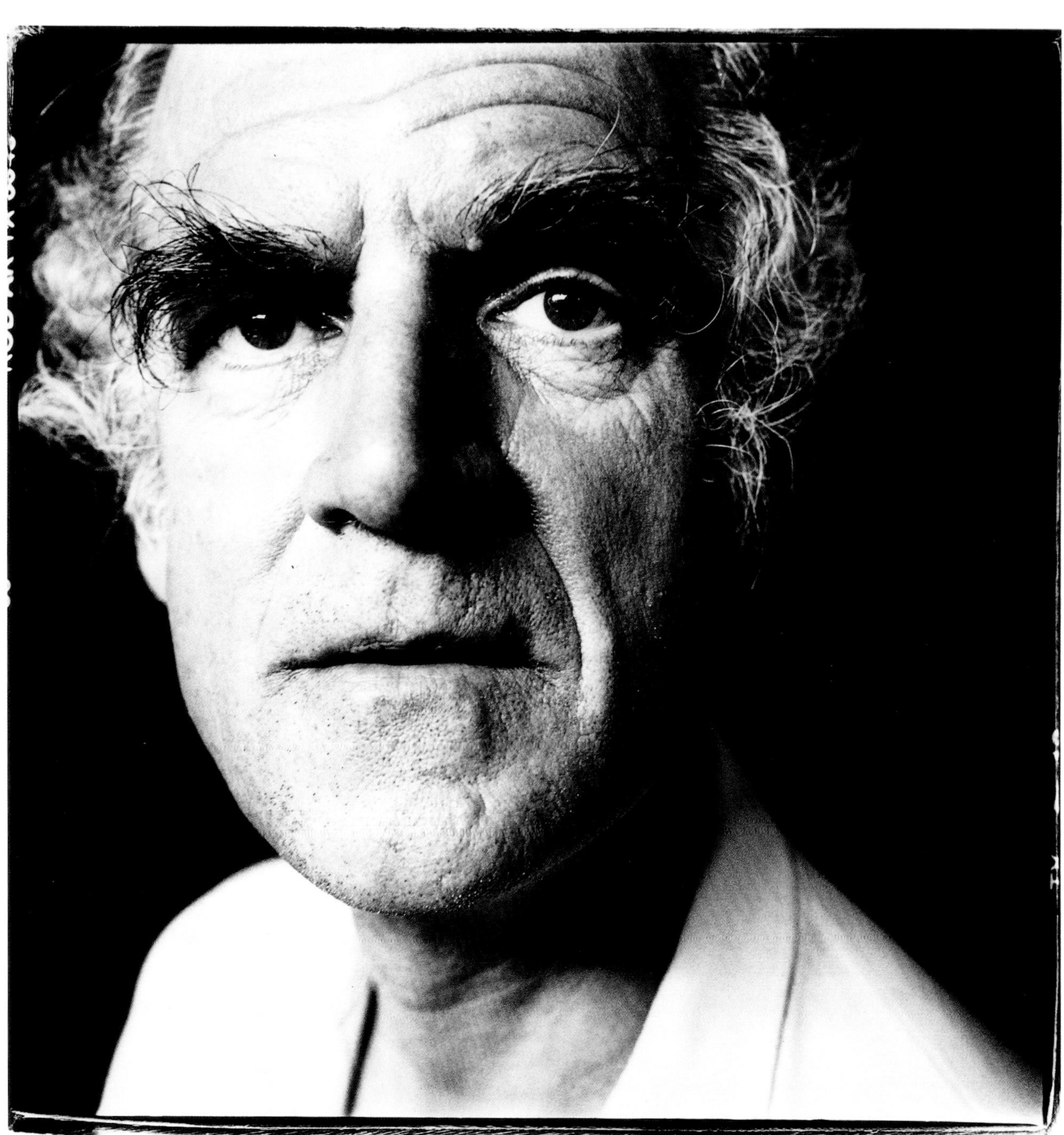

**Professor Dr Michael Theunissen**

*Berlin, 4 November 1991*

"Originally influenced by Heidegger I later became interested in Kierkegaard, phenomenology from Husserl to Sartre, German idealism, critical theory and – for some years now – in early Greek thought. Main subjects: intersubjectivity, dialectic and dialogue, negation and negativity, time, philosophical fundamentals of psychopathology, problem of metaphysics, question of the possibility of [a] philosophical theology."

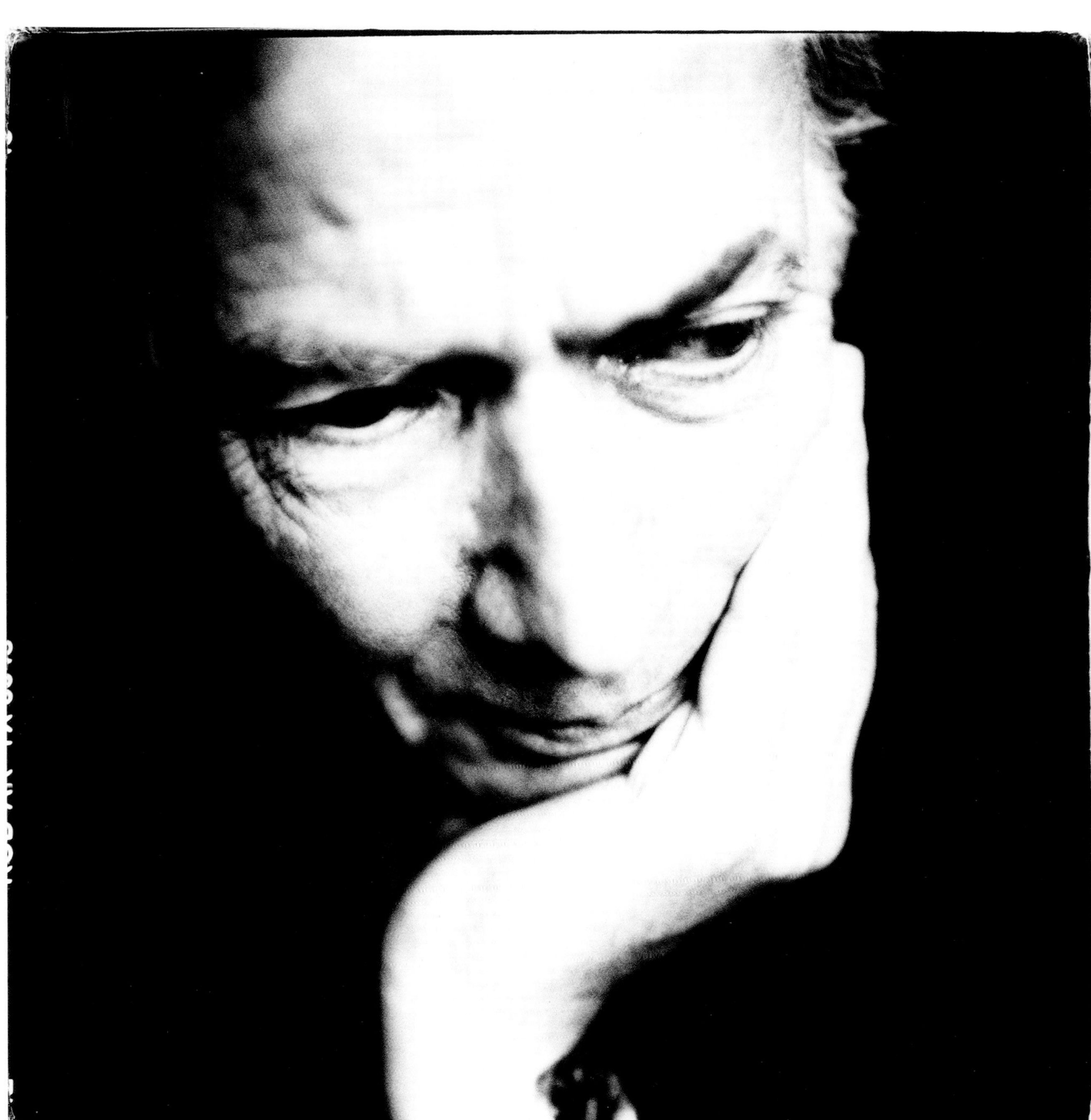

**E P Thompson**

*London, 30 May 1989*

"I am seeking to rescue the poor stockinger, the Luddite cropper, the 'obsolete' hand-loom
weaver, the 'utopian' artisan, and even the deluded follower of Joanna Southcott, from the
enormous condescension of posterity." *'The Making of the English Working Class', 1963*

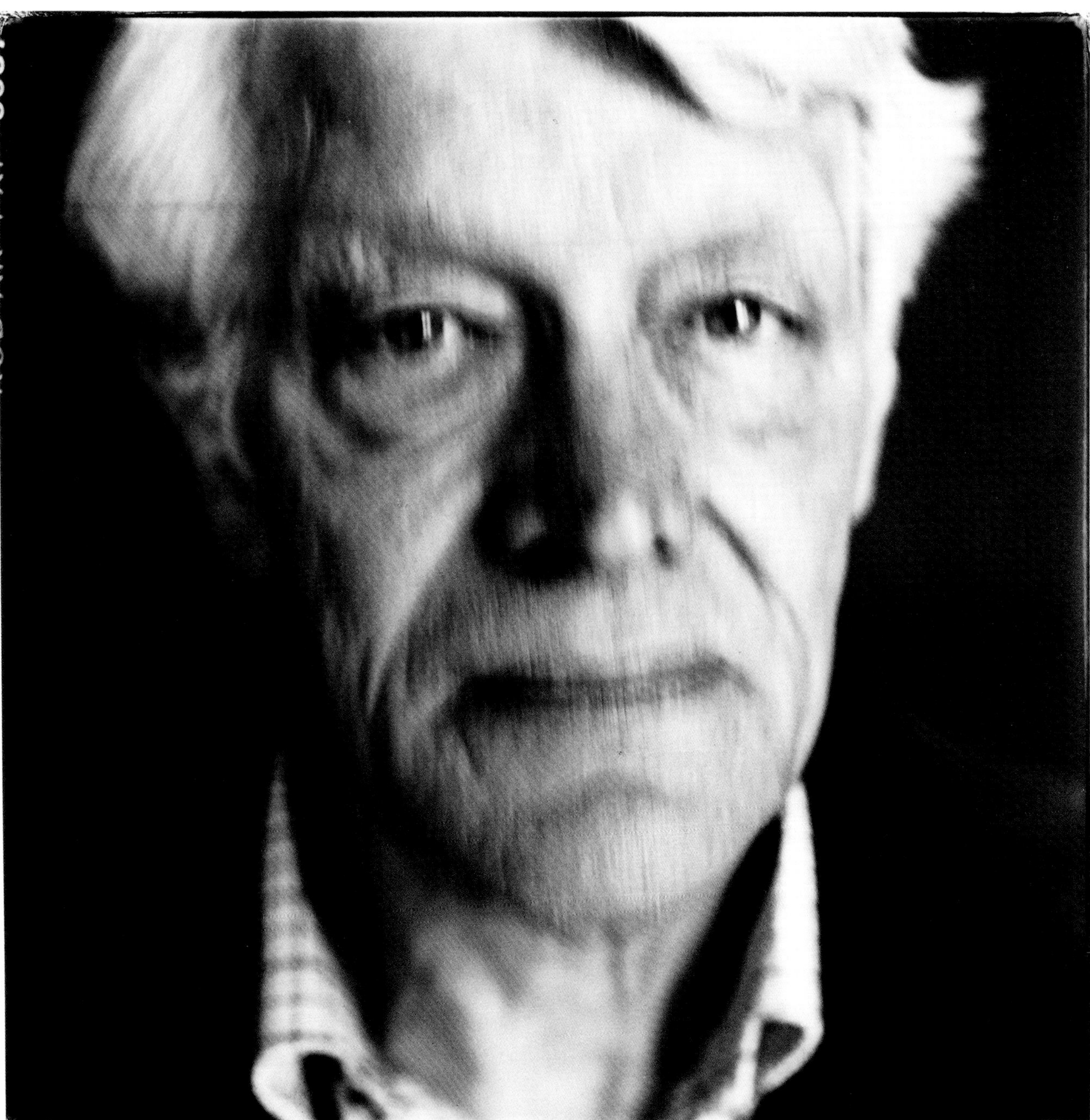

**Professor Tzvetan Todorov**

*Paris, 7 December 1991*

"Wisdom is neither hereditary nor contagious: one attains it more or less, but always and only alone, not by virtue of one's membership in a group or state. The best regime of the world is never anything but the least bad, and even if it is the one under which we live, everything still remains to be done."

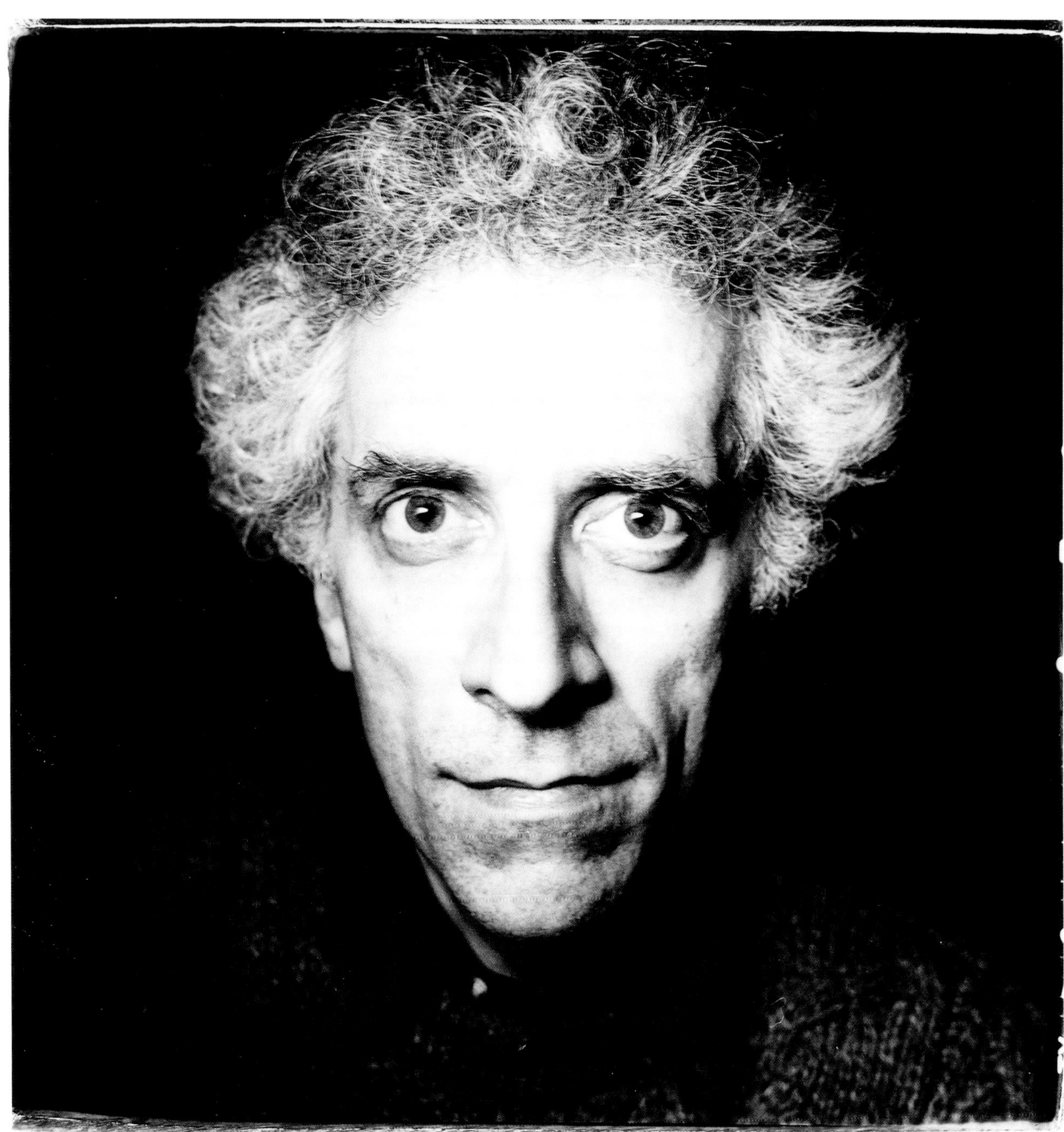

**Professor Ernst Tugendhat**

*Berlin, 4 November 1990*

"Philosophy is not a profession but a way of looking, doubtfully and with a sense for the important. Philosophy is, today, not a pastime. It is inescapable, because we no longer believe to know what is good and, as Socrates said … 'Knowing begins with knowing that one knows not.' We moderns are unable to sneak out of the moral point of view, yet there is nobody who tells us what it is."

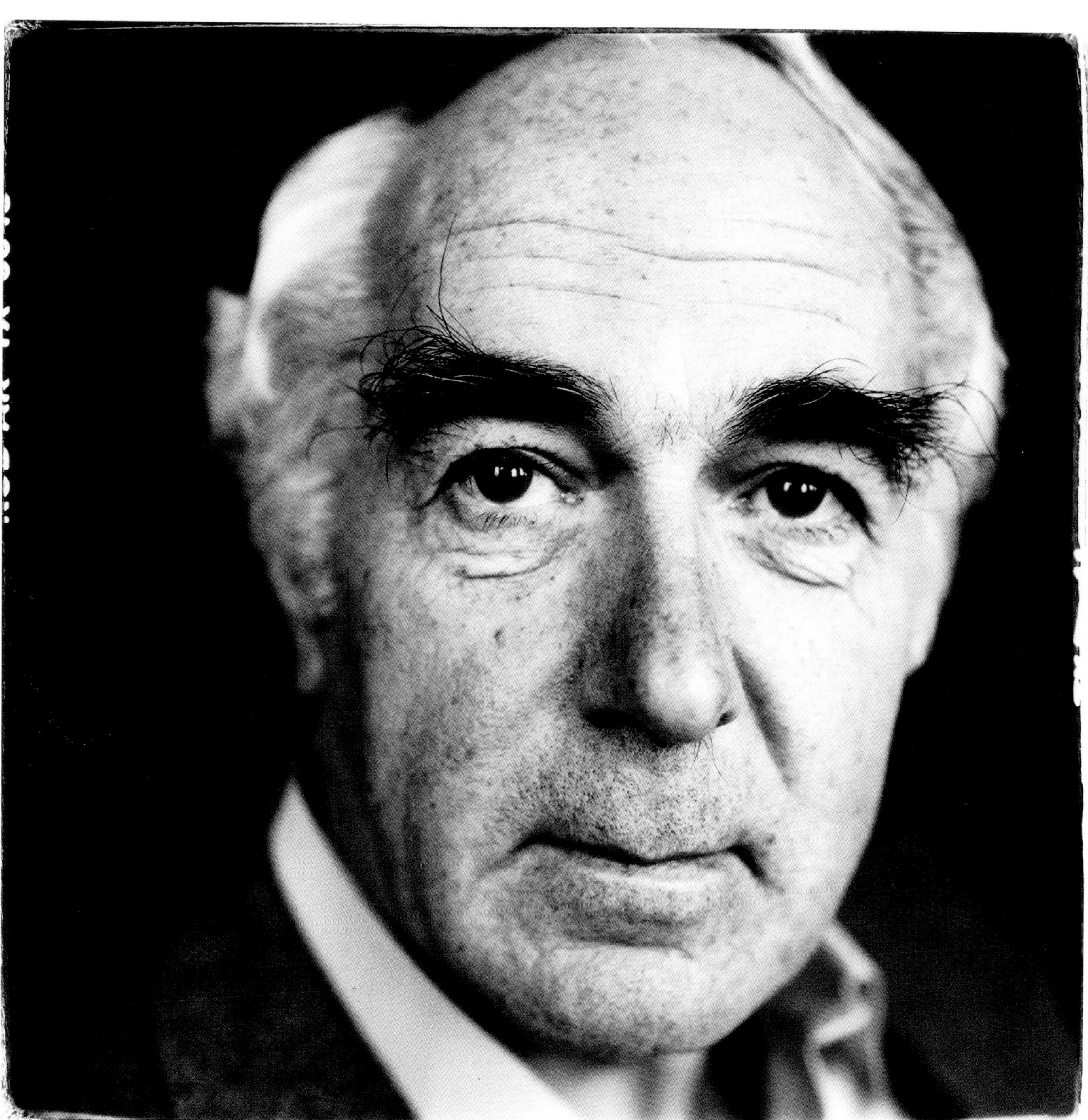

**Sir Geoffrey Warnock**

*Oxford, 5 July 1990*

"To be clear-headed rather than confused; lucid rather than obscure; rational rather than otherwise; and to be neither more, nor less, sure of things than is justifiable by argument or evidence. That is worth trying for."

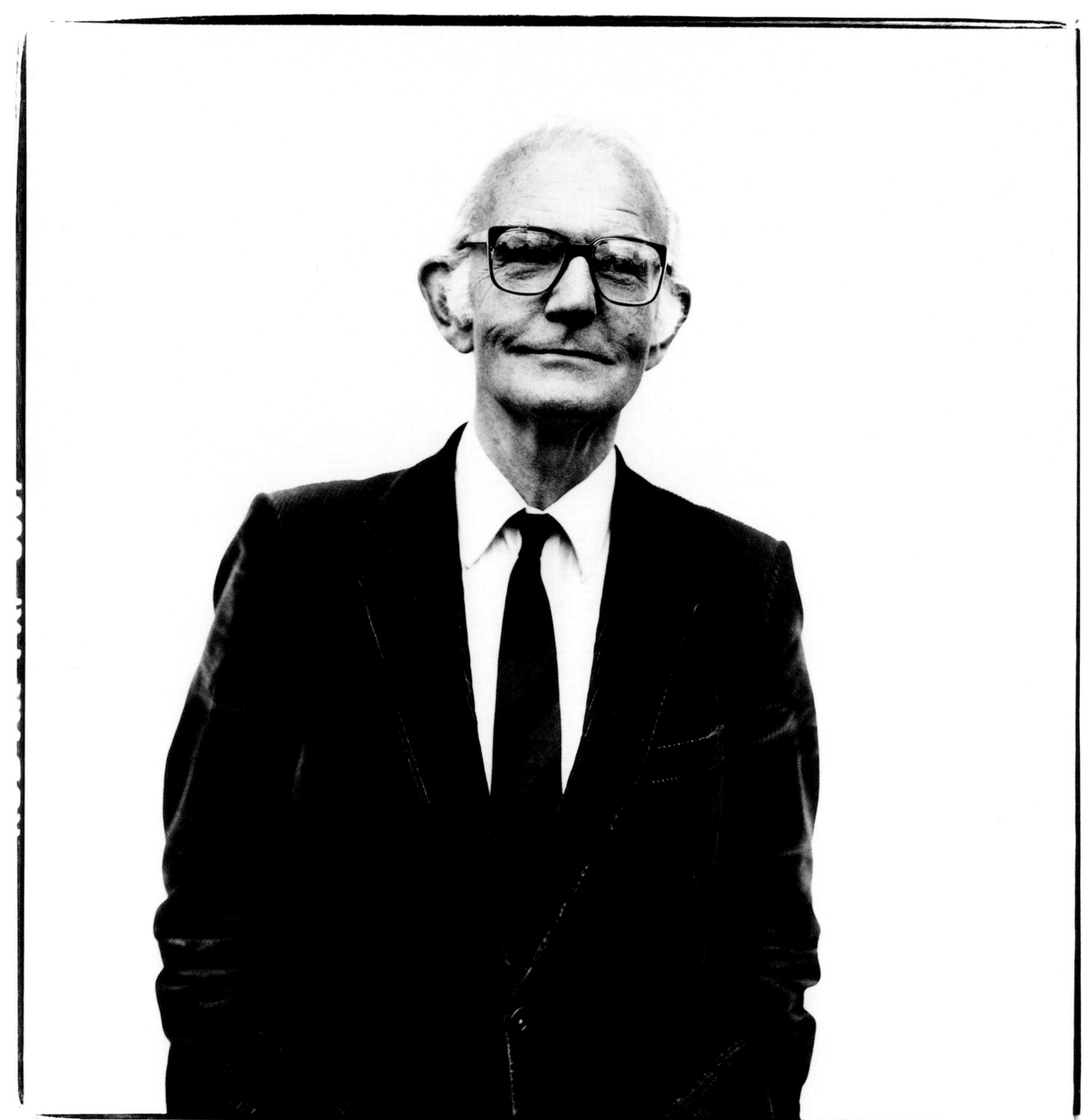

**Baroness Mary Warnock**

*Oxford, 5 July 1990*

"The point of philosophy, in my view, is to examine things we take for granted in ordinary or scientific discourse, such as the nature of causal connexion, the relation between mind and body, or health and disease. Philosophy has always been concerned with such hidden meanings, so it has been of especial interest to me to try to understand and expound the writings of previous philosophers, Aristotle, Hume or Sartre, as a means to this philosophical end."

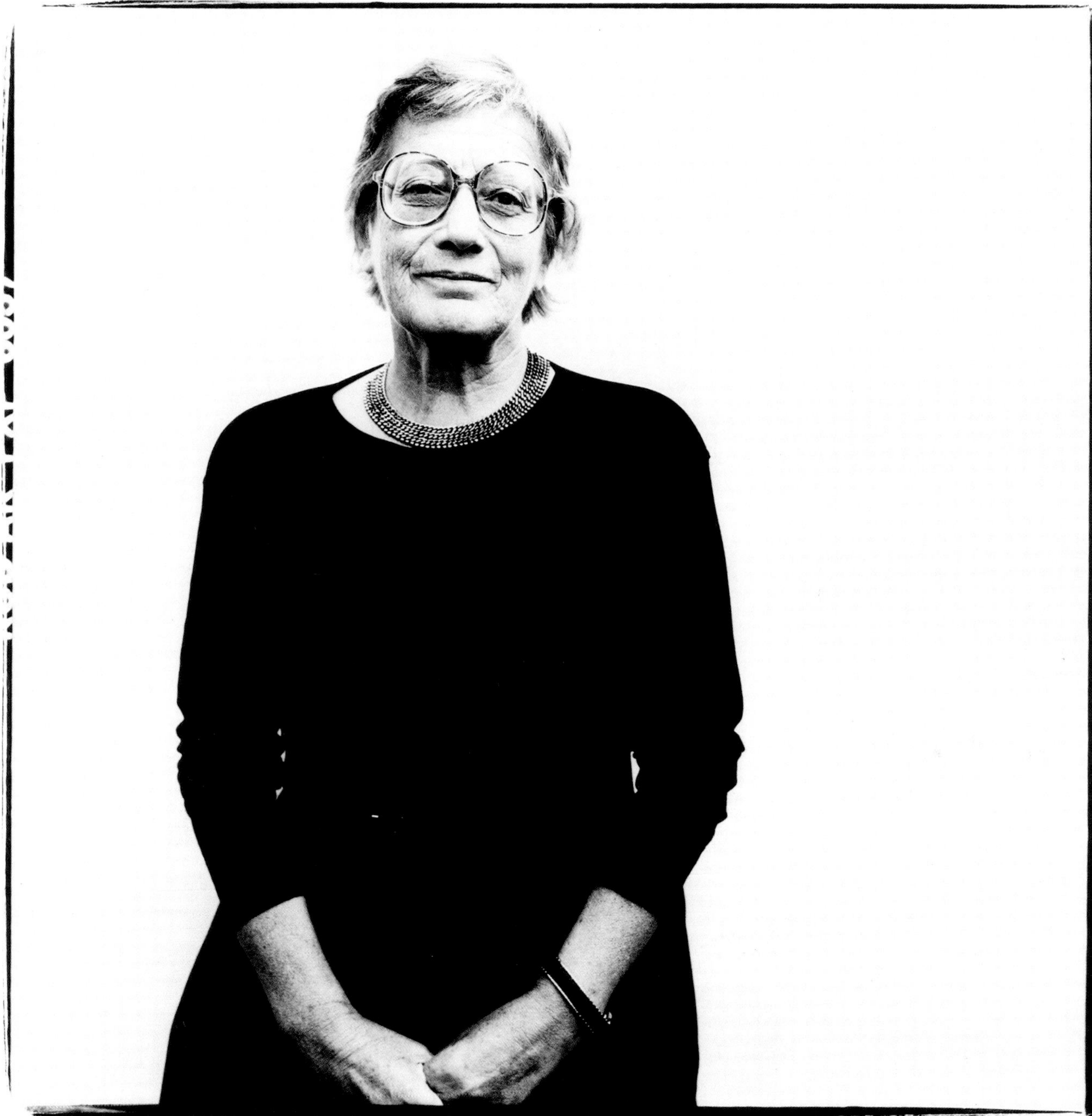

**Dr David Wiggins**

*London, 4 September 1990*

"Philosophy will break out of its own accord wherever people wonder what they are, or what they are aiming at and why, or whenever they try to make real sense of the thoughts that they find themselves with. This is to say that it is part of ordinary life. If someone says he dispenses with all metaphysics and wants none, you will be wise to expect him to be bogged down in a metaphysic so poor that, if it were explicitly revealed, you would not know whether to laugh or cry.

At different times, different questions give trouble and provoke philosophy. Professional philosophers may be justly expected not only to confront the questions that press upon their times and to help their students to do so, not only to persevere in the ancient struggle against the forces of error, confusion and fraudulent reduction, but to keep the archive; to serve as a (however unwanted) dialectical conscience and memory for their society; to show, by deliberating them, that ends as well as means can be deliberated; to show, by example, that it is possible, by an extreme effort, to hold more than two pertinent ideas in the mind at one time."

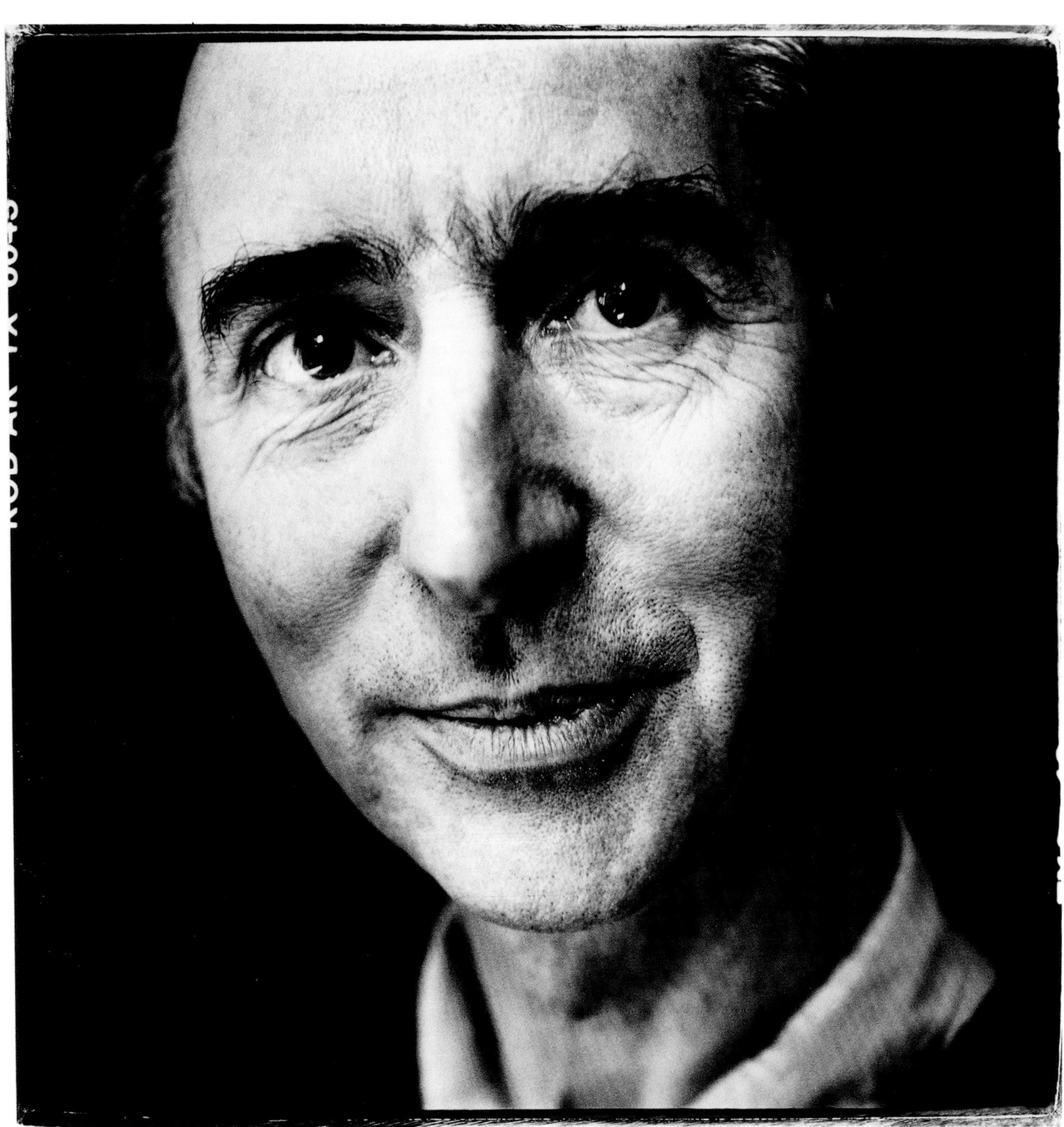

**Professor Bernard Williams**

*Oxford, 23 August 1990*

"I am interested in ethics – both in what it has been and in what it might become. Ideas of the ancient Greeks concern me, because if we understand them better, we can use them in trying to understand ourselves. My main aim: to see how philosophy might help us to develop the new ethical ideas we certainly need."

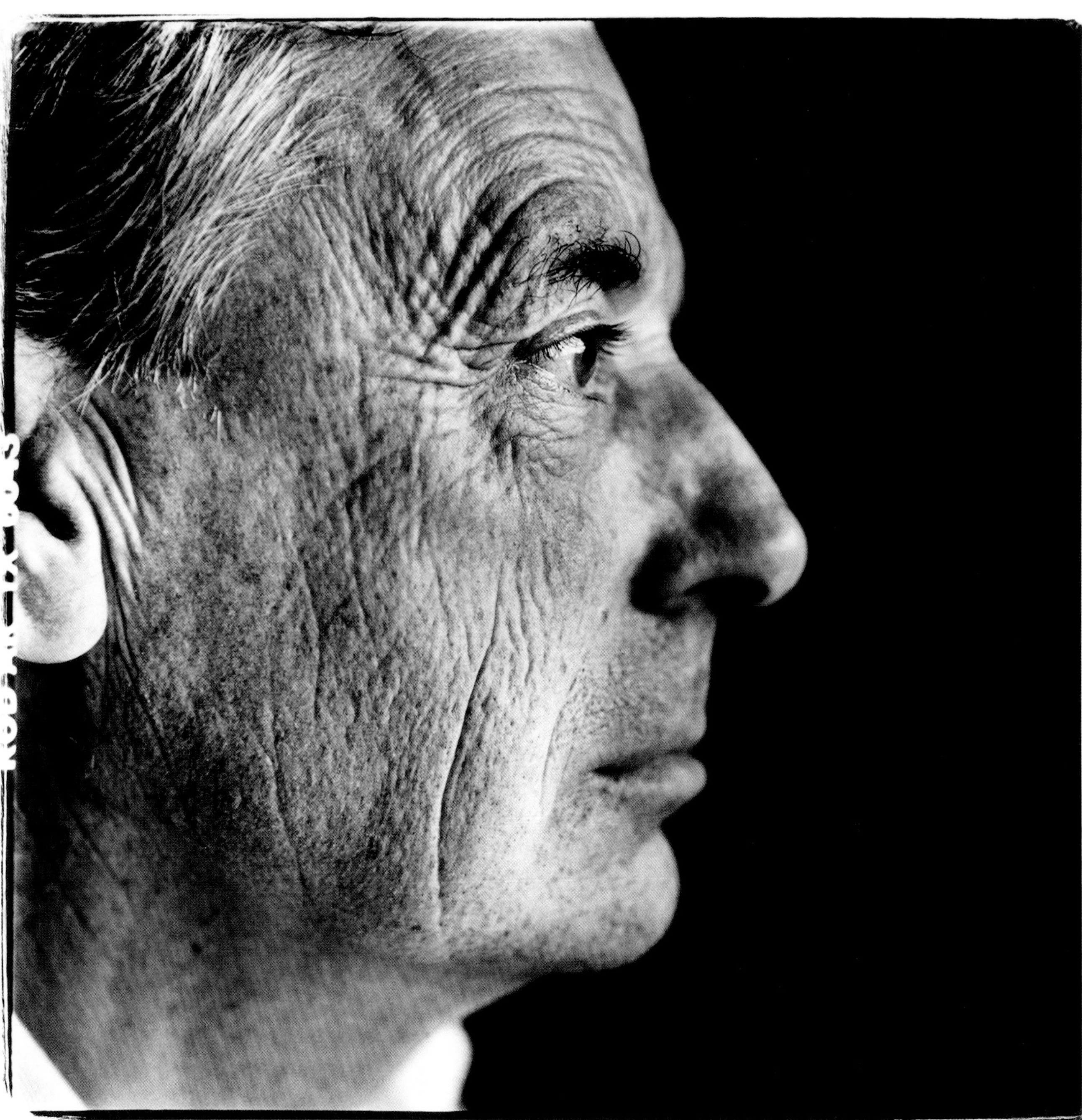

**Professor Dr Ursula Wolfe**

*Berlin, 4 November 1991*

"The big question behind philosophy is: what is the good human life. But that doesn't mean that, as a philosopher, you have to pose this question directly or that you could give substantial answers. Nor does it imply that the philosophical life will be happier than other forms of life."

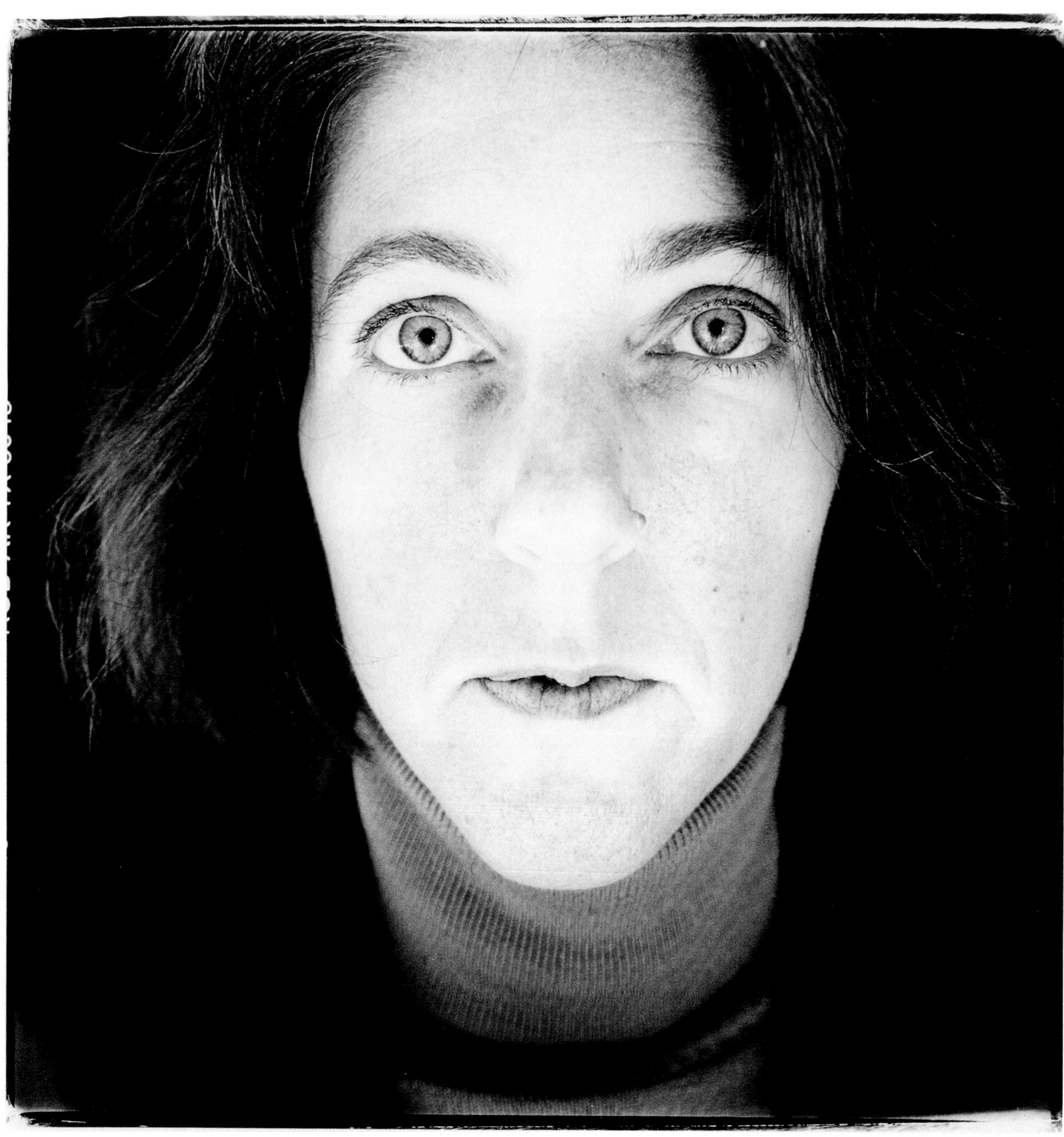

**Professor Richard Wollheim**

*London, 4 July 1990*

"Philosophy is for me mostly a form of self-knowledge."

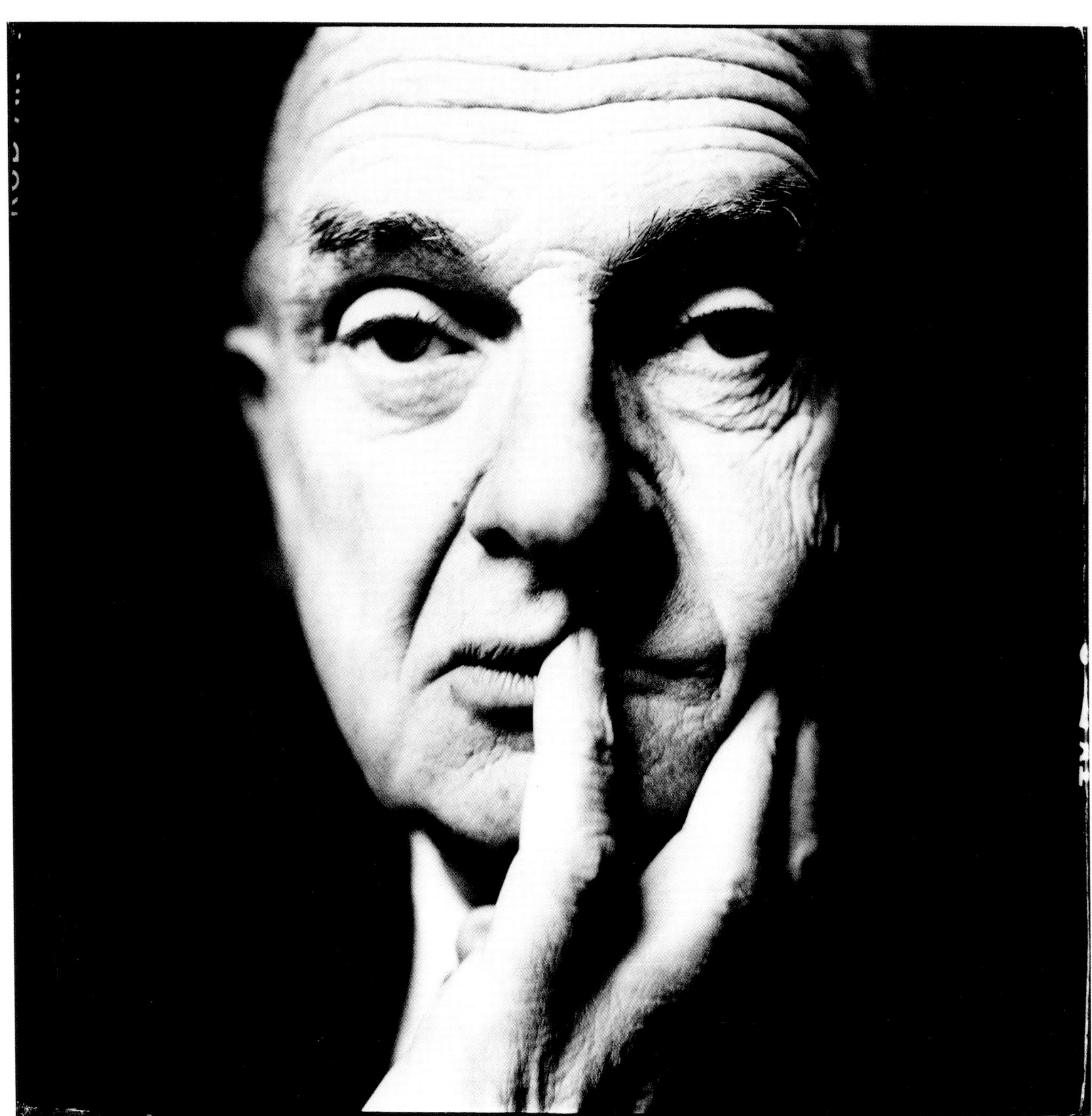

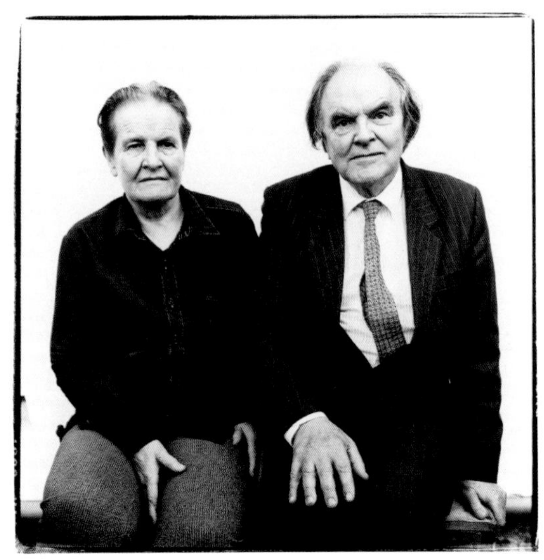

**Professor Elizabeth Anscombe and Professor Peter Geach**

*Cambridge, 15 May 1990*

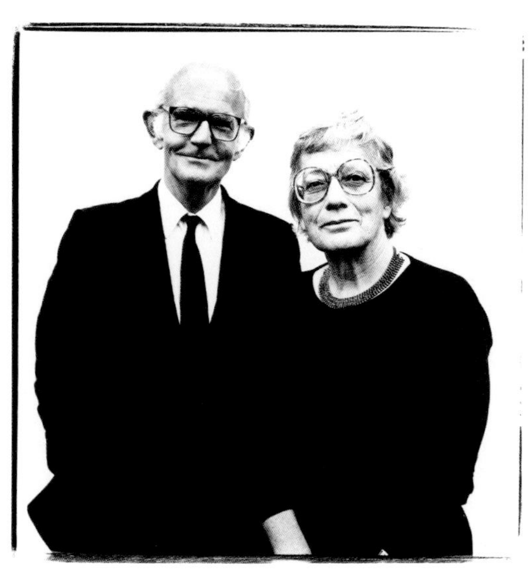

**Sir Geoffrey Warnock and Baroness Mary Warnock**

*Oxford, 5 July 1990*

**Thanks to**

Tom Ang, Zelda Cheatle, Simon Chu, Rob Dawson Moore
Gavin Fernandes, Colin Ford, Robin Gibson, Vince Goodsell
Greg Hobson, Shirin Homann, Ted Honderich
Suzy Hudson, Chris Jones, Sylvie Languin and all at Rapho
Dewi Lewis, Steve Mayes and all at Network
Catherine Robinson, Geoff Sapsford, Dani Steele
Jane Sutton, Damon Thomas, Volker Wolfe